The Potted Tree
Essays in Venetian Art

Norman E. Land
28 Dec. 2019

Norman E. Land

THE POTTED TREE

ESSAYS IN VENETIAN ART

Missouri Center
for the Book

ಿಿ ಿ

Missouri Authors
Collection

CAMDEN HOUSE

Published by Camden House, Inc.
Drawer 2025
Columbia, SC 29202 USA

Printed on acid-free paper.
Binding materials are chosen for strength and
durability.

ISBN:1-879751-85-2

Library of Congress Cataloging-in-Publication Data

Land, Norman E., 1943-
     The potted tree : essays in Venetian art / Norman E. Land. -- 1st
ed.
          p.   cm.
     Includes bibliographical references and index.
     ISBN 1-879751-85-2
     1. Painting, Italian--Italy--Venice. 2. Painting, Gothic--Italy--Venice.
     3. Painting, Renaissance--Italy--Venice. 4. Painting,
     Baroque--Italy--Venice. 5. Color in art. 6. Imagery (Psychology)
     I. Title.
     ND621.V5L25   1994
     759.5'31--dc20   93-40775
                                                                          CIP

Contents

For
my mother
Dorothy Whetstone Land
and
in memory of my father
Norman Earl Land

List of Plates

List of Plates

Acknowledgments

WHEN FIRST WRITING AND THEN while revising the essays gathered together here, I received assistance in various forms from a number of people whom I should like to thank. First and foremost is Paul Barolsky, who introduced me, when I was a graduate student in the McIntire Department of Art at the University of Virginia, to the beauties of form and subject matter in Venetian art. Indeed, these essays may be said to have their beginnings in his seminars as well as in informal discussions with him about William Hazlitt, Walter Pater, John Ruskin, Kenneth Clark, Sydney J. Freedberg and the *tradizione legitima* in general. Moreover, he read early drafts of almost all of the essays and made numerous helpful suggestions for their improvement.

Over the years that these essays have been in progress, I have had the good fortune to receive various kinds of assistance from a number of other friends and colleagues whom I should like to thank. They are Andrew Ladis, Anne Barriault, Paul Hills, Edwin Muir, Michelangelo Muraro, David Summers, David Carrier, Philipp Fehl, Patricia Meilman, David Rosand, and William E. Wallace.

I am deeply grateful to Charles R. Mack for his interest in this book, for his many invaluable suggestions for its improvement, and for agreeing to write a foreword to it.

I should also like to thank the editors of the journals in which earlier versions of some of these articles were originally published for permitting me to include them here. The introduction (originally with Paul Barolsky as co-author) first appeared in *Studies in Iconography* 9 (1983): 57–65; chapter 1 in the *Konsthistorisk tidskrift* 55 (1986): 47–53; chapter 2 in the *Southeastern College Art Conference Review* 9 (1989): 299–304; chapter 3 in *Artibus et Historiae* 10 (1984): 61–6; chapters 6 and 7 in *Art History* 13 (1990): 293–317; and chapter 8 in the *Southeastern College Art Conference Review* 11

Acknowledgments

(1987): 114–9. All of the original essays have been corrected and all have been expanded, though some more so than others, and where necessary revised in the light of recent or previously overlooked publications.

A grant from the Research Council of the University of Missouri helped to defray some of the costs of publication.

I am especially indebted to the Art Department of Memphis State University for awarding me the Dorothy K. Hohenberg Chair of Excellence in Art History (1992-1993); this honor allowed me time to prepare the manuscript for publication. The Hohenberg fund also covered some of the costs of producing this book. During my stay at Memphis State University, I received valuable support from my colleagues, especially Professor Carol Purtle, and from my assistant, Gillian Harris.

While in Memphis, I also benefitted from the keen insight and encouragement of Patricia P. Bladon, Assistant Director of the Memphis Brooks Museum of Art. I am forever indebted to her and to her son, Patrick, who made me laugh.

My dear friend and confidante Allyn Elizabeth Holladay gave me her support and assistance just when they were most needed, and I owe her more than I can say.

By far my greatest debts are to my daughter, Elizabeth and my son, William, for their humor, understanding, and confidence in me.

FOR WELL OVER A DECADE Camden House has been establishing a widely respected reputation as an academic publisher. Its managing editors have solicited volumes from some of the best scholars in the areas of German, Scandinavian, British, and American literature and criticism and in literary criticism and history in general. Those of us concerned with the history of art should, therefore, gladly welcome Camden House's venture into our discipline with the publication of Norman Land's volume of essays centering around the appreciation of Venetian art. When the first chapters for *The Potted Tree* were sent to me, as Art History Editor for Camden House, I soon realized that the book would make not only a valuable addition to the publisher's catalogue but also a significant contribution to the critical approaches of my discipline.

The appearance of *The Potted Tree* is especially welcome, for it occurs at a time in which the practice of art history is undergoing enormous changes. Upon the traditional art historical systems of formal analysis and iconographical interpretation have been grafted most of the contemporary trends in critical theory — textual analysis, cultural anthropology, semiotic interpretation, Derridadaist deconstructionism, and all sorts of shadings of the New Historicism. To a discipline that admittedly had grown atrophied in its methods, these sorties from across the borders often have been refreshing and provocative, but at the same time disturbing. When applied to art historical situations, these critical imports have yielded a mixed bag of scholarship. Too often in the New Art History, the work of art itself is treated more as artifact than as art, with the unfortunate result that our discipline frequently appears on the verge of losing its integrity. Land's approach offers an alternative method that does much to recapture the sublime experience of visual dialogue.

Two days before I wrote this preface, an editorial in *The Art Bulletin* (September 1993) had reminded me of what all the new scholarly approaches to art history had sacrificed. Richard Brilliant recounted a story of an undergraduate halted at the crossroads of career choice. Her heart tells her to become an art historian but she is fearful that the discipline is so clogged with critical method that she cannot do so "without risking the lessening of the pleasure she has in looking at works of art." Sadly, the story ends with the student choosing another course of graduate study, in part because, if she does so, "she can continue to go to museums and art galleries for pleasure, without the burdensome interference of current art-historical discourse." Had she only been able to read Land's *The Potted Tree*, Brilliant's imaginary (but nonetheless real) student might have found the courage to have followed her heart!

In part, what Norman Land does is to revive the "antiquated" procedure of visually experiencing a work of art. It is a method that I do not, personally, follow in my own writing but which I try to do in my looking and, occasionally (but, alas, too infrequently) do when examining objects with my students. Land allows the work of art to give him pleasure and even joy. Certainly anyone who enjoys art and has an imagination does this, but the practice, lamentably, is vanishing in the way in which our generation is instructing the next. We seem afraid to show emotion, as if feeling must preclude erudition.

Brilliant's editorial, however, ends with a statement of hope, one that predicts the present volume: "Perhaps in the regeneration of the ekphrastic mode, more poetry than prose, we can find a model for making works of visual art speak to and through us." And it is in the "ekphrastic mode" that this book is composed — what might be loosely described as a viewer-response approach. *The Potted Tree* renews and expands upon the grand tradition of looking, feeling, and experiencing that, for example, Walter Pater had used when, more than eighty years ago, he evoked the vision of Leonardo and Giorgione. Norman Land offers a gracefully constructed framework for visual rapture and allows us to listen with our eyes.

Charles R. Mack
Professor of Art History and
William Joseph Todd Professor of the Italian Renaissance
The University of South Carolina
Columbia, 6 October 1993

Preface

ALTHOUGH WRITTEN INDEPENDENTLY of one another, the following essays are interrelated and together form a kind of history of Venetian painting from the early fifteenth to the eighteenth century. Each essay deals with one of two topics and sometimes with both. These topics are *colorito*, which has to do with the naturalistic imitation of nature and which is customarily identified as a salient feature of Venetian art, and *fantasia*, which, as far as I know, has never been singled out as a consistently significant aspect of Venetian art, except by Giorgio Vasari. Over and above those topics, the essays are united by a concern for the ends of art. Indeed, together they constitute an outline of the history of the criticism of Venetian painting from the Renaissance to the present. An important aspect of that criticism is imagination exercised within certain limits or contexts.

Some comments about the means employed in these essays would seem in order, for a single approach has not been used throughout. The introduction, although it discusses meaning in Giorgione's *Tempest* (plate 1) is also a kind of credo that lays out some of the assumptions I have made in the essays that follow it. In short, I argue that form is as important to the meaning of a work of art as subject matter. This is certainly not a new argument, but one that needs to be periodically restated, for the practice of the interpretation of form is too often disregarded, possibly because it is usually confused with the kind of formalist criticism that, say, Roger Fry sometimes employed.

In chapter two, focussing on Michele Giambono's *Saint Michael Archangel* (plate 2) in the Bernard Berenson Collection at Villa I Tatti, I attempt to come to terms with the essential quality of the artist. Some scholars might dismiss this sort of essay as old-fashioned because it is an example of the kind of writing that, say, Berenson might have attempted (and certainly with far greater success). But since the quality and value of Giambono's art has never been properly described, it seemed necessary to write about him and his paintings in this manner.

Four of the essays are more or less in the vein of iconographical interpretation established in this country by Erwin Panofsky, but in them I have been attentive to more than symbolism and subject matter. I have also given attention to the relation of form to content and at times have employed evocative description as a means to that end. One of these studies deals with meaning in one of Nicolas Poussin's self-portraits (plate 31). This chapter may seem out of place here, but one of its themes is the French artist's debt to Venetian coloring, a debt that many other seventeenth-century painters shared. The essay, then, intends to demonstrate the vitality of Venetian painting of the Renaissance during a period when the art of the Lagoon was, relatively speaking, at a low point.

There are two chapters dealing with the alleged "limitations" of ekphrastic or evocative description as it was practiced in the sixteenth and seventeenth centuries. In these chapters I have analyzed how critics responded to one of Titian's greatest paintings, the now-destroyed *Martyrdom of Saint Peter Martyr* (plate 27), in order to demonstrate that imagination was the foundation of that response. In another essay, I interpret anew a well-known document concerning a famous painting by Paolo Veronese, focussing on his *fantasia* and its relation to the Venetian tradition of artistic license.

The chapter on Lorenzo Lotto's *A Maiden's Dream* (plate 20) requires special comment, for in it I have gone beyond accepted art historical practice, employing a poetical method like that of, say, Adrian Stokes in his *Stones of Rimini*, or Robin Ironside in some of his essays. Many art historians agree that much in Venetian painting is not subject to understanding by rational means. If this is so, then scholars may either ignore the poetic in Venetian art because it is not subject to conventional art historical methods, or find some other way to express that "poetry." Following the lead of such scholars as Theodor Hetzer, Philipp Fehl and Sydney J. Freedberg, I have chosen the latter course because the poetry in Venetian art remains one of its most vital attributes, and because I believe that it is not necessary for art historians to repudiate a kind of writing that has proven itself to be well-suited for dealing with the poetic in art.

1: Introduction — Meaning in Form

THE REASONABLE PROPOSITION underlies current scholarship in art history that to understand a work of art objectively is both interesting and valuable. To be objective, art historians attempt to understand the meaning of works of art through the complex social, political, economical, artistic, theoretical, and literary factors that shaped their creation. As commendable as this underlying approach is, and as attractive as the results of contemporary research are, the possibility of a complete understanding of a work of art remains debatable. Not only is the past too complex for us to grasp fully and firmly, but also our interpretations, however scientifically objective we may try to make them, are always colored by our "subjectivity," by our own inescapable and insurmountable sensibilities, tastes and biases. This objection to the claim of objectivity among art historians will be seconded by those conversant with the history of art history. For they know that interpretations will change from generation to generation and ultimately depend upon the particular intellectual, spiritual and social circumstances that inevitably influence the interpreter.

We should add something more in this regard: although we continue to accumulate factual data, we do not necessarily advance in our understanding of art and its history. Indeed, art historians would be hard pressed to defend the claim that today we have a better historical understanding of quattrocento and cinquecento art than Giorgio Vasari had over four centuries ago.

A prominent scholar has recently observed that "the [art] historian is not a critic and should not aspire to be one."[1] This remark, it seems, in spite of its grammatical form, is less an injunction as to what art history should be than a description of what it is at present. Many art historians prefer to separate criticism from history, to

---

[1] Ernst H. Gombrich, *The Sense of Order: A Study in the Psychology of Decorative Art* (Ithaca, 1979), 305.

make a distinction between the subjective basis of criticism and the reputedly objective basis of history. Certainly that which a work of art originally intended or meant is different from its significance to us. Nevertheless, the history of interpretation is the history of changing emphases on what is significant in the work of art. What is of significance in it to one generation is often a matter of indifference to another, for the interpreter of art is able to illuminate only facets of a work, never its totality. And the determination of significance, even if based upon an historical sense of what the work of art intends, rests upon critical judgment, whether that judgment be made consciously or not.

The foundation of critical history remains Vasari's *Lives of the Artists*, and since he wrote, Winckelmann, Diderot, Ruskin, Baudelaire, Pater, Berenson, and others, have written brilliantly and memorably about art, never with complete detachment, yet in ways that are important and valuable to us and to our response to art. We still see Michelangelo's work through the eyes of Vasari; we gain insight into Chardin's paintings from Diderot; and Baudelaire has much to show us about Delacroix's art. These writers were, to be sure, partisans, and made their critical judgments, by in large, without claim to universal validity. They passionately embraced the virtues of great artists, allowing those virtues to inhabit their imaginations, and their observations have endured. Even though some scholars have ridiculed the "appreciation" of art, all writing about art, explicitly or not, is appreciation. Writers are attracted to their subject because they appreciate some value in it — formal, illustrative, or moral. And, like it or not, all writing on art is "impressionistic." No matter how dispassionate writers about art try to be, their work will always reflect, to one degree or another, the impression made upon them by that art. For example, a recent interpretation of Giorgione's *Tempest* (plate 1) is based upon the author's undeniably strong impression that the picture is "strange" and "haunting" and "filled with fear and foreboding," which "mood," in turn, bears "an uncanny resemblance" to that of Venice in 1509.[2]

No one will deny that the subjectivity of the critical historian can, and very often does deepen and enrich our understanding of

---

[2] Deborah Howard, "Giorgione's *Tempesta* and Titian's *Assunta* in the Context of the Cambrai Wars," *Art History* 8 (1985): 275–7. See also Paul H. D. Kaplan, "The Storm of War: the Paduan Key to Giorgione's *Tempesta*," *Art History* 9 (1985): 405–27.

art and culture. For instance, because of his temperament, Walter Pater was drawn to the idealism and erotic content of Plato's writings, and although his own view of Platonism is idiosyncratic, it informs his interpretation of the Neoplatonic influences on Italian art. Literary historians have studied Pater's achievement, but art historians generally have been wary of his impressionistic approach. Pater's understanding of Neoplatonism in his book *The Renaissance*, however, not only foreshadowed modern scholarly recognition of this important topic, but influenced it directly. Until recently, this influence for the most part has escaped the notice of art historians.[3]

Since the end of the nineteenth century art history has been skeptical of criticism, of subjectivity, but perhaps it is not skeptical enough, putting too much faith in its own objectivity. The lack of sufficient skepticism is especially evident, for example, in social and political histories of art. This kind of art history often isolates some possible causes of art, invariably refusing to acknowledge that historical reality, beyond one's capacity to know it fully, is more complex than historical explanation allows for. Sometimes, too, historians invoke the word "proof," a term better employed by mathematicians than by students of human events, and they are often unaware of their moralizing tone.

A similar lack of caution is found in iconographical scholarship, which has also been dominant in the current practice of art history. Many art historians believe that if they find the text on which a work of art is based — the "right text" — they will discover the intention of a work of art. Even though we have theoretical models for determining intention in art, it is disputable, as observed above, whether we can fully understand intention. Moreover, students of iconography sometimes do not acknowledge that their own temperaments contribute to their discovery of the supposed "right text." There is also a gap between written word and visual image that can never be completely bridged by interpretation. We may find the particular text that a painting illustrates, but the painting, we should always remember, is not its equivalent, for the

---

[3] For an excellent discussion of Pater and his influence on modern art and thought, see Paul Barolsky, *Walter Pater's Renaissance* (University Park and London, 1987).

former is a visual image, the latter is verbal.[4] At best, we can say that the painting is an analogue of the text or that it approaches the text. But we may not claim that the text and the painting are equal, that meaning in the painting is exactly that of the text. Certainly, the text will help us to approximate meaning in a work, but we cannot correctly say that it explains the meaning.

Most scholars agree that meaning is inseparable from the form in which it is expressed, but they too often say little or nothing about the form of a painting or sculpture. There are entire books and articles in art history focusing on iconography that, in effect, are elaborate and often learned commentaries on literature and history, but which do not even attempt to describe works of art. That is to say, those commentaries do not attempt to explore the relation between the work of art's form and its subject or to explain the ways in which form expresses meaning. It can even be argued that if not described, the work of art is not interpreted. Because we usually associate intelligence primarily with verbal skills, we too often ignore the kind of intelligence that resides in form, the intentions of form, which are part of the work's total meaning.

Too often, we make no distinction between the qualities of a work by, say, Marco Basaiti on the one hand and Giovanni Bellini on the other. In other words, a *Madonna and Child* by Bellini, even though it were precisely the same in subject matter, attributes, and symbols as one by Basaiti, would not mean the same. We might say that the soul of each artist leaves its own indelible mark — that which the Renaissance called *aria* — in the forms and colors of the work.

The literature about Giorgione's relatively small, but enormously vital panel, the *Tempest* (plate 1), which takes its title from a sixteenth-century description, provides an excellent illustration of how art historians in general approach art. Some scholars have identified the figures in this painting as classical gods or Biblical heroes and saints. Others have suggested that it represents a moral or cosmological allegory. However, none of these interpretations has gained wide acceptance, possibly in part because they depend, as is usual in modern iconographical studies, on interpretations of

---

[4] For similar observations, see Wendy S. Sheard, "Giorgione's *Tempesta*: External vs. Internal Texts," *Italian Culture* 4 (1983): 145–58.

literature, and not on an understanding of the painting as such.[5] Many have come to believe that the meaning, if not the value, of the *Tempest* resides solely in the matter of its illustration. The painting is treated as if it were a literary work, and we are expected to "read" it as if it were a text or an approximation of a text. The distinguished scholar, Johannes Wilde, best summed up this kind of thinking when he observed of the *Tempest*: "Not until the actual text on which a picture such as this was based has been found can we claim that we understand its subject."[6]

In reaction to the excessive literalism of iconographical exegesis, other scholars have suggested that Giorgione's painting (plate 1) is actually a "non-subject" or even an "anti-subject" and this has been a helpful corrective to a fundamental fallacy of interpretation.[7] But in so doing, they have overreacted because pictures still have subjects even if they cannot be associated with texts. Briefly stated, the subject of this panel is a man and a nude woman with a child in a landscape overshadowed by dark clouds, with thunder (no doubt) and a bolt of lightning. The question of what this subject intends or expresses is another matter.

Tracing the great tradition of creative writing about art back to the times of Giorgione himself, we find that, while acknowledging the relations of art to literature, this writing has treated painting as painting, not misleadingly as literature and has had much to say about the "subject" of art as art (not necessarily its literary content). The respect for the meaning of art as it resides in form is everywhere evident in the writings of Vasari and is exemplified in his brief description of a lost painting by Giorgione:

> He painted a nude man with his back turned, and he had on the ground a most limpid stream of water in which he made the reflection of the front part: on one side was a burnished cuirass, which he [i.e., the figure] had taken off and in which

5 For a review of the extensive literature on the *Tempest*, see Salvatore Settis, *La "Tempesta" Interpretata: Giorgione, i committenti, il soggetto* (Turin, 1978), 46–81. See also idem, *Giorgione's "Tempest": Interpreting the Hidden Subject*, trans. Ellen Bianchi (Chicago, 1990), 48–80.

6 Johannes Wilde, *Venetian Art: From Bellini to Titian* (Oxford, 1974), 66.

7 See especially Creighton Gilbert, "On Subject and Non-Subject in Italian Renaissance Pictures," *Art Bulletin* 34 (1952): 202–16.

was his left profile because in the polished surface of that
armor every thing was seen clearly; on the other side was a
mirror in which there was the other profile of the nude.[8]

As Vasari tells us further, this work was made to demonstrate the
virtuosity of painting, which surpasses three-dimensional art in its
capacity to show in one scene more views of nature than is possible
with sculpture. The picture, however, was more than the mere illustration of the *paragone* of painting and sculpture, for on the basis
of our knowledge of the artist's extant works, we can easily imagine
both its mimetic power and the sensuous beauty of light reflecting
from the water, armor, and mirror to which Vasari alludes.

The Venetian art historian and theorist, Marco Boschini, remarked in the seventeenth century that the forms in Giorgione's
paintings "lucono come specchi" ("sparkle like mirrors"), and this
luminosity is part of the subject of the *Tempest*. In modern art literature, one of Vasari's heirs, Walter Pater, above all remarks upon
the significance of form to painting, especially in the work of Giorgione and his school:

> that the mere matter of a picture, the actual circumstances of
> an event, the actual topography of a landscape — should be
> nothing without the form, the spirit of the handling, that
> this form, this mode of handling, should become an end in
> itself, should penetrate every part of the matter: this is what
> all art constantly strives after, and achieves in different de-
> grees.[9]

---

[8] Giorgio Vasari, *Le vite de' più eccellenti pittori, scultori ed architettori*, ed. Gaetano Milanesi, 9 vols. (Florence, 1906), 4:98 (hereafter cited as Vasari-Milanesi): "Dipinse uno ignudo che voltava le spalle ed aveva in terra una
fonte d'acqua limpidissima, nella quale fece dentro per riverberazione la
parte dinanzi: da un de' lati era un corsaletto brunito che s'era spogliato, nel
quale era il profilo manco, perchè nel lucido di quell'arme si scorgeva ogni cosa; dall'altra parte era uno specchio che drento vi era l'altro lato di quello
ignudo..." (Unless otherwise noted, all translations are my own.) See also
Paolo Pino, *Dialogo della Pittura* in *Tratatti d'arte del Cinquecento fra manierismo e contriforma*, ed. Paola Barocchi, 3 vols. (Bari, 1960), 1:131(hereafter
cited as *Tratatti*), who first told the story of Giorgione's painting.

[9] Walter Pater, *The Renaissance*, ed. Donald L. Hill (Berkeley, Los Angeles
and London, 1980), 106.

The ostensible subject of the *Tempest* is a landscape with three figures, be they personifications of gods, saints, or mere mortals. A description or explication of its purported symbolism does not give a full sense of the painting's meaning and value, for it does not comment upon the indissoluble relation of form to content. The "essence of the pictorial," to borrow a phrase from Pater, resides in the obliteration of the distinction between form and matter; and the union of form and matter, that which gives the *Tempest* its vitality, should be addressed, not overlooked, as we search for the artist's "reading list" or that of a possible advisor or patron.

In Giorgione's painting (plate 1), we gaze upon a rich, green landscape, permeated by a moist, dark blue-green atmosphere. In the distance is a city, its towers and dome rising above the horizon; in the middle ground looms a pool of water spanned by a bridge; closer still are trees and bushes on either side; part of a ruin and a wall with broken columns are to the left; and in the foreground a man, dressed as a courtier and holding a staff, stands on one side of a stream, which extends forward from the pool towards a nude woman suckling a child. Two slow-moving rhythmic undulations of form intersect toward the lower center of the picture. One of them descends from the ruin on the left, to the wall with columns, to the earthy patch below the woman, and as it does so, the forms of the ruin are softened by its arches and by the gently bending trees and bushes. This movement interweaves with the flow from the tree above the woman through the bushes adjacent to her, across the rocky mound of earth upon which she is seated, to the other side of the stream. These two descending curves are soothing in their easy, graceful, turning cadence.

The grace of circularity may be said to inform the painting. The trunks and branches of the trees on either side of the pool bend centerward, implying a circular form at the upper center of the picture, harmoniously and gently enframing the distant city and the pool of water. At the left of the stream, the courtier is gracefully posed. Bending fluidly, his body is echoed by the line of the bank of the stream at his feet, and echoed again by the shapes of the bushes behind, as by the large, semicircular flow of form from the right side to the upper left of the painting. Giorgione's landscape *fantasia* reveals further circular resonances. The tops of the broken columns implicitly unite with the decorative circles of the ruins, and these columns, which circle in depth, imply a relation to the male figure, who, leaning forward and holding his arm behind him, is, so to speak, a personified cylinder. Beyond the columns, the bank of the stream curves alluringly into the distance, reaching the dome, the shape of which is consonant with the curving forms of the architecture in the middle ground. Even straight lines approximate curves; for instance, the ruin behind the courtier is ever so slightly at an oblique angle to him, combining with the figure not to sustain a purely upward flow, but to suggest the sweeping curve of the composition. The vertical aspect of the pictorial design is diminished somewhat by the inflection of the courtier's staff set at a slight, inward angle, approximating that of the analogous slender, bending tree behind him. Without his staff, the courtier would be less unified to the landscape, for in the distance the lightning ultimately sustains its form.

Part of the pleasure of the *Tempest* resides in the discovery, upon repeated return to it, of further secrets of its harmony. Closer scrutiny may be given to the complexity of the trees, which are united not only to the figures before them, but are no less integrated with the figure on the side of the canvas opposite them. We shall recognize, too, in the bend and sway of the grass and trees rhythms that further harmonize this vision, and we shall find that the bridge in the middle of the painting — one of its primary actors — is slightly tilted, contributing to the subtle upward movement previously observed.

The harmony of the painting depends fundamentally on Giorgione's rendering of light and color. Lights and darks are subtly harmonized to create a unified, nearly palpable atmosphere. Almost as in a painting by Velázquez, this atmosphere seems a living presence, and although we do not fully perceive its nuances, we see the overall pattern of lights and darks shot through the landscape. The pale, pebble-filled sand is played against the dark foreground stream; this shaded area corresponds to the blackened blue-green mass of the bridge's watery shadow and to the darker areas of the trees on either side. Yet in these plants, as in the sky above and in the grass below, golden light plays upon surfaces, brightly animating this subdued vision of lush blue-green.

A single passage may serve to illuminate the refinement of Giorgione's handling of light and color. Red and white are interwoven throughout the courtier's costume, harmonized by his pink leggings and subdued by their gold, which is related also to the golden threads of light scattered brightly through the obscurities of the landscape. Although enshadowed, his left leg emerges luminous at the calf, a subdued variant of his white blouse, brilliant against the red and coal black shadow of his cape. Few painters have matched Giorgione's uses of black and white (or whitened luminous color). The vibrant white of the blouse is wed to the even brighter white of the woman's drapery. These two brightened areas are, in turn, linked to the flash of lightning above; and touches of white — flecks upon the water and upon the faces of the buildings — serve to integrate these areas. The building at the far right, beyond the woman, is a luminous, yet partially shaded variant upon her whiteness, while the columns just behind the courtier are similarly analogues to his leg in both their subdued darks and whites and their cylindrical forms. Here we witness the effortless, modulated unison of light, color, and form upon the picture's surface.

The pleasingly intricate harmonies of the *Tempest*, inseparable from its ostensible subject, are intimately wed to its meaning. We have been gazing upon the harmonious relations of man, woman, and child in nature, figures made alluring by virtue of the richness of the very form rendering and uniting them. The man's dress implies the harmony of court-dweller with nature, and the wholeness of nature, with which he and the woman are united, is expressed by the appearance of the four elements — earth, air, water, and the fire of the lightning — all interpenetrating in Giorgione's vision. Inspite of the flash of lightning and the impending storm, the figures are reassuringly aloof and calm, and perhaps the most soothing image is that of the child at his mother's breast, an illustrative metaphor for the formal epiphany of ease, security, comfort, and oneness that the artist has made visible. For, in effect, our relation to the painting and to the world it so convincingly represents is analogous to the child's relation to his mother. The flash of lightning and the broken columns evoke the idea of the passage of time in this illusory space, but, in the same moment, Giorgione presents us with the image of an eternal order, gentle yet vital, to which we happily often return. And the pleasure we take in this nurturing harmony does not lie merely in the idea of such, which is but a cliché; rather it resides in the subtle and complex realization of that idea as form.

Scholars have associated the *Tempest* with texts by Ovid, Statius, Petrarch, Boccaccio, and Francesco Colonna, author of *Hypnerotomachia Poliphili*. They have identified the work as an illustration of Adam and Eve, the discovery of Moses, the legends of Saint Roch and Saint Theodore, and as a profane rest on the flight into

Egypt. Jupiter, Bacchus, Paris, and Danaë have all been identified as protagonists of the picture, and it has further been supposed that Giorgione depicted the origins of the Vendramin family, a lament on the death of Matteo Costanza, and a portrait of his own family. In more general terms, the painting is said to be an illustration of the union between sky and earth; an allegory of the four elements; an allegory of charity and strength overcoming fortune; and a visualization of the dictum: *Harmonia est discordia concours*. None of these interpretations has received wide acceptance; most have been generally discarded.[10] And yet, if we reflect upon them, although they are too literal, we see that many are both interrelated and, more importantly, responsive to the painting.

The classical, Biblical, and allegorical interpretations all hark back to the mythic or primordial, to the sense of something momentous and extraordinary — the very origins of things — as if in many interpretations, Giorgione is implicitly thought to have recreated the origins or early history of humankind and nature as an harmonious ideal. Whether seen as a representation of Adam and Eve, of the Holy Family, of the origins of the Vendramin, or of Giorgione's own family, the painting, as scholars have repeated over and over in different ways, expresses an ideal of familial harmony, as if it captures a prelapsarian wholeness, Biblical, pagan, or both. These interpretations are of a piece with those allegorical readings that stress unity or concordance, and although it may not be reasonably claimed that all of these interpretations fit together, there is a certain family relation or correspondence among them. For all of their literalizing distortion, they may be retained as metaphors, not only for what they reveal about the history of taste and attitude during the last century or so, but for what they point or allude to in the painting itself. Certainly, the narrowly conceived goal of explaining pictures with texts results in the apparent falsification of those works, or fictionalizing of them, but, nevertheless, there is a certain truth in the unwitting historical fictions about the *Tempest* — a truth rooted in the scholar's original apperception of Giorgione's splendid, harmonious vision. The scholar's falsifying iconographical interpretation, then, is a metaphorical analogue of the painting.

---

[10] The various interpretations here referred to are discussed by Settis, *La "Tempesta,"* 46–81 and idem, *Giorgione's "Tempest,"* 48–80.

This recognition goes against the grain of accepted dogma in art history, as reflected, for example, in the writings of Erwin Panofsky, who has been widely followed in his belief that

> since the inward experience of the art historian is not a free and subjective one, but has been outlined for him by the purposeful activities of the artist, he must not limit himself to describing his personal impressions of the work of art as a poet might describe his personal impressions of a landscape or of the song of a nightingale.[11]

Although Panofsky was correct to say that the work of art "outlines" our response to it, the distinction he draws between poetry and reputedly scientific scholarship is false, and the recent intense criticism of Panofsky's own brilliant hypotheses would suggest, in the negative sense of his distinction, that in his various Neoplatonic interpretations he himself lapsed into "poetry."[12] Some of his "poetry," in a positive sense, is sound and helpful, and although his Neoplatonic interpretation of the Medici Chapel, for example, has been harshly dealt with in recent years, its concern with certain aspects of the work still calls our attention to some of its significant features (such as the intricate movement of the architecture heavenward) even if, strictly speaking, the chapel does not illustrate philosophical doctrine. His interpretation, like readings of Giorgione's painting, is rooted in a perception of the work of art, inspite of itself and inspite of what the work becomes or is made into in iconographical exegesis.

As critics, art historians interpret art implicitly, rendering not an interpretation of the object unto itself and apart from the impression they have of it, but rather giving their impression of it. The distinction between intention and critical response exists only in theory, never in practice. The history of the history of art teaches this. Modern scholarship has been generally hostile to the kind of "impressionism" advocated by Pater, described by him as part of the course of interpretation, and followed here in describing the *Tempest*. The distinction should be made not between "intention"

---

[11] Erwin Panofsky, "The History of Art as a Humanistic Discipline," in *Meaning in the Visual Arts* (New York, 1955), 20.

[12] For example, see Frederick Hartt, *Italian Renaissance Art*, 3rd ed. (Englewood Cliffs, 1987), 543.

and "significance," but between the degrees of convincingness in diverse impressions of art. This is not to say that art historians should blithely ignore historical fact; indeed, their explications are stronger in direct proportion to their knowledge of the facts. But analysis of the *Tempest*, or of any other work of art, is never, can never be, of fact itself, but transcribes a "sense of fact." In recent years a number of methods or approaches has been adopted by art historians to the study art — not only iconography and art theory, but contextualism (the study of art in its social, political, economic, and other contexts), structuralism, semeiotics, and post-structuralism. All of these methods are either helpful or potentially so, but in the end, none of them undermines interpretative impressionism, which rather than being a weakness is still, when practiced well, indeed poetically, art history's greatest strength.

2: Melancholic Fantasia

ONE OF THE MOST ENGAGING Venetian artists of the first half of the fifteenth century is Michele Giambono, or Michele di Taddeo di Giovanni Bono, to give his full name. The exact date of Giambono's birth is not known, but he must of been born in or around the year 1400. The first known document concerning him, dated in November of 1420, reveals that he was then already a painter, married, and living in the *sestier* or parish of Sant'Angelo. He may have come from a family of painters originating in Treviso, but we cannot be certain of that, for when he signed his mosaics in the Mascoli Chapel in the church of San Marco,Venice, he identified himself as *venetus*. Seemly most of his life was spent in Venice, although he certainly sent his work to other towns and cities and probably travelled at least as far south as Fano on the eastern coast of Italy. He seems to have been highly regarded by his contemporaries and may have had a reputation for fairness and honesty. These traits of character are suggested by the fact that he was on several occasions called upon to arbitrate disputes, one of which occurred in 1453 and involved the payment to be made to the great Florentine sculptor Donatello for his magnificent equestrian statue of Gattamelata in Padua. Another time, in 1430, he and other artists, possibly including Pisanello, were called upon to place a monetary value on a now-lost painting of Saint Michael in the church of San Michele in Padua by Jacopo Bellini, who, interestingly enough, belonged to the same *scuola* as Giambono. The last known documents to mention the artist are dated 1462, and he must have died in or shortly after that year.

Although Vasari apparently knew nothing of him, from the sixteenth century until about the middle of the nineteenth, he was primarily recognized as the artist responsible for some of the mosaics in the Mascoli Chapel in the church of San Marco, Venice. He is widely known now, however, as an accomplished painter on panels. Much of the responsibility for this change in the artist's reputation is due to Bernard Berenson, who was among the first to

notice his importance in the history of Venetian painting: "until
we are able so to differentiate Giambono from his compeers as to
have a precise idea of his career and quality, our knowledge of the
beginnings of modern painting in Venice must remain in the hazy
state in which it is at present."[1]

A number of scholars, dismissing several spurious attributions
and offering convincing new ones, have more or less established
the artist's authentic works. Moreover, the outlines of his career
are somewhat more distinct than they were in Berenson's day. Still,
a precise idea of the quality of Giambono's work remains elusive,
due in part, ironically, to Berenson's own rather slight evaluation
of the artist.[2] Indeed, there is further irony here, for Berenson
possessed one of Giambono's most impressive works, his engaging
Saint Michael Archangel (plate 2), painted, it seems, in 1440 for the
church of San Michele in San Daniele in Friuli and still one of the
finest of the considerable pleasures at I Tatti. Unfortunately, the
San Michele altarpiece (originally containing both painted panels
and carved figures) to which this painting belonged, is now dispers-
ed.[3]

In Giambono's painting (plate 2), Saint Michael, crowned with a
slender diadem of raised and gilded gesso and wearing a flowing
dalmatic of dark crimson and gold, sits on what appears to be a back-
less throne of Gothic design, which is altar-like in its construction.
With an expression of an infinitely tender sadness, the Archangel
gently inclines his head towards his right hand in which he holds a
gilded orb surmounted by a monstrance, symbol of Christ's rule in
the universe through His crucifixion and resurrection and the re-

---

[1] Bernard Berenson, *Venetian Painting Chiefly before Titian at the Exhibition of
Venetian Art*, The New Gallery (London, 1895), 6.

[2] For recent studies of Giambono's art and further bibliography, see Norman
E. Land, "The Master of the San Marino 'Saints' and Other Followers of Michele Giambono," *Acta Historiae Artium* 28 (1982): 23–38; idem, "Michele
Giambono's 'Coronation of the Virgin' for S. Agnese in Venice: A New Proposal," *Burlington Magazine* 119 (1977): 167–74; and idem, (as in note 3
below).

[3] For a reconstruction of this altarpiece and that of another centered around
the *Seated Male Saint* now in the Ashmolean Museum, Oxford, see Norman E.
Land, "A New Proposal for Michele Giambono's Altarpiece for S. Michele in
S. Daniele in Friuli," *Pantheon* 4 (1981): 304–9; and idem, "A New Panel by
Michele Giambono and a Reconstructed Altarpiece," *Apollo* 119 (1984):
160–5.

enactment of those events in the Holy Eucharist. With his left hand the Archangel points heavenward to the source of his vanquishing power — in the original altarpiece, the Virgin and Child. On the front of Michael's dalmatic and echoing his gesture, a tiny, half-length figure of Moses points upward to Christ, who, here represented as the Man of Sorrows, stands in an open sarcophagus. He is crucified yet resurrected; dead, yet triumphant over death. At the very top of the panel, two angels of an order apparently less than that of the archangel descend through the eternal blue empyrean and outward on either side of him along golden rays of light, bringing with them sword and scales, instruments of the Last Judgment, while below, the gently undulating folds of Michael's costume cascade from his knees to his feet and there envelop the bestial archdemon, who forever writhes in convolutions of evil and sin.

In the presence of the delicate beauty of the *Saint Michael*, it is surprising to recall that critical evaluations of Giambono's panel paintings are of relatively recent origin and even more surprising to learn that they tend to be rather negative. For example, Crowe and Cavalcaselle felt that the artist "never freed himself from the grotesque rugosity peculiar to the Veneto-Byzantines," and they pointed to a lack of "correct" drawing in his figures.[4] For Lionello Venturi, all of Giambono's works display a little "coarseness," and the artist lacks "originality."[5] Berenson noted an absence of "backbone" and "relief" in the painter's figures, which he characterized as "toothless, limpid and wooly."[6] According to Giuseppe Fiocco, the artist did not possess "the instinct of an innovator or a particle of the heroic spirit."[7] Raimond van Marle, echoing previous judgments, held that Giambono lacked originality, that his art lacks "substance," and that he was a docile imitator of other artists.[8]

Giambono's style as manifested in, for example, the Berenson panel (plate 2) is, indeed, fundamentally decorative and not sub-

---

[4] Joseph Archer Crowe and Giovanni Battista Cavalcaselle, *A History of Painting in North Italy*, 2 vols. (London, 1871), 2:13.

[5] Lionello Venturi, *Le origini della pittura veneziana* (Venice, 1907), 93–94.

[6] Bernard Berenson, *Venetian Painting in America* (New York, 1916), 5.

[7] Giuseppe Fiocco, "Michele Giambono," *Venezia* 1 (1920): 236.

[8] Raimond van Marle, *The Development of the Italian Schools of Painting*, 19 vols. (The Hague, 1926), 7:378.

stantive. His forms are always linear and almost completely flat, and he does not hesitate to embellish his panel quite freely with embossing and gold-leaf. His figures are often not in a single scale; there is hardly ever any spatial depth in his paintings; and the perspective of objects — in the case of this panel, that of the throne — is never drawn with mathematical accuracy. Furthermore, the strong similarity of some of Giambono's forms to certain ones in works by Lorenzo Veneziano, Jacopo and Pierpaolo dalle Masegne, Gentile da Fabriano, Pisanello and Jacopo Bellini is very striking, and one keenly senses his profound debt to those artists. Still, one feels that the criticism of Giambono's art has been not so much inaccurate as inappropriate, because implicit in that criticism is the theory that holds the proper function of art to be the naturalistic imitation of nature, a theory which, to be sure, informed the art of the Renaissance proper, but which evidently is not related to the Venetian master's paintings.

Clearly other criteria are needed for the appropriate evaluation and appreciation of Giambono's work, and one way of establishing those criteria is through an understanding of Cennino Cennini's treatise, *Il libro dell'arte*, which was written in or around the year 1400, when the author, who was a Florentine painter, resided in Padua.[9] Although there is no evidence that Giambono was directly influenced by Cennini's book, nevertheless, it seems reasonable to assume that the two artists worked in a similar workshop-tradition and that Giambono held ideas about, or attitudes towards, art similar to those expressed by the Florentine. In any case, various aspects of the Venetian's paintings suggest as much.

Although Cennini explains his ideas about art briefly and none too precisely, we find after careful study of his text a coherent, unifying thought. He begins with a broad explanation of the historical and theological context within which the artist works. In the beginning God created heaven and earth, and He created man and woman in His own image, giving them every virtue, "tutte virtù." Then Adam and Eve fell and were driven from paradise, a circumstance that forced Adam to discover by means of his "scienza" the need to find a way of making a living by the use his hands. The meaning of the word "scienza" changes according to the context in which Cennini employs it, but here he seems to mean what

[9] Cennino Cennini, *Il libro dell'arte o trattato della pittura*, ed. Fernando Tempesta (Milan, 1975), 8–9. (Hereafter all references to Cennini's text are to this edition.)

Leonardo da Vinci called "discorso mentale," that is, reason. Be that as it may, "scienza" refers to some sort of mental activity in contrast to a manual one, and in his description of Adam and Eve after the Fall, Cennini connects mental activity and manual labor, a connection that foreshadows and parallels his description of the painter's operations.

After the time of Adam and Eve, mankind pursued many different occupations, not all of which are of equal value because some are "di maggiore scienza" and *scienza* is more worthy than manual operations; in other words, some occupations are more purely mental activities than others and are therefore more valuable. Close in rank to work that is purely mental is the art of painting, which combines a foundation of *scienza* and operations of the hand. Here *scienza* seems to refer to, not reason, but another kind of mental action, *fantasia*, for Cennini goes on to say that painting combines "fantasia" and operations of the hand. He also explains that the end or goal of that combination is to discover "cose non vedute" ("things not seen"), things "cacciandosi sotto ombra di naturale" ("hiding under the shadow of the natural"). The artist, Cennini explains, is one who sets forth "quello che non è," and he must fix or form "that which does not exist" in his art. This reference to "things not seen" is somewhat obscure, but, as David Summers has so convincingly explained, Cennini "should perhaps be understood to mean that the forms of nature 'figure' or 'shadow forth' both higher truth and that which the painter makes visible in his art. In this case sensory objects would both suggest high truth *and* stimulate the *fantasia*; and painting...draws close to poetry."[10]

Those things that hide themselves in "the shadow of the natural" are revealed by means of the mental activity called "fantasia" in combination with particular manual skills. For that reason, as Cennini tells us, in art's eternal hierarchy, painting should be crowned and honored as poetry is. The poet with his "scienza prima" is free to compose and to bind together according to his will. Similarly, the painter is free to compose, for instance, a standing figure or a seated one, as he pleases, according to his *fantasia*. We should note that *fantasia* here refers to the ability to invent and compose images, but it also refers to memory, the capacity of the mind to store and to recall images.

Having established the primacy of the mental activity called

10 David Summers, *Michelangelo and the Language of Art* (Princeton, 1981), 493 note 90. (Author's emphasis.)

"fantasia," Cennini, employing a mixed metaphor, tells the young draftsman that his "most perfect guide" is the "triumphal portal of drawing from nature." We should not, however, construe this advice to mean that the artist is always to draw directly from nature, for Cennini explains that constant drawing with a pen will make the artist a skillful expert and will give him the ability to draw from images in his head, "entro la testa sua"; that is to say, the practice will give him the ability to draw from memory.

According to Cennini, the operations of *fantasia* are memory and invention, but, as he also explains, it has another function, especially for artists who want to find their own style. He says that after diligently copying the works of the best masters, if the artist has been granted a "punto di fantasia," a modicum of imagination, he will eventually find his own manner. *Fantasia* in this case is the mental action or quality that transforms the slavish copying of another's work into a personal style.

Cennini briefly describes what today we would call a "creative process." The artist studies nature in order to fill his *fantasia*, specifically his memory, with images, and he copies the work of a master in order to find a style in which to show forth those images. When he sets about to paint, he recalls those images or invents new ones by combining two or more. These recollected or invented images are not like the original objects as they were observed in nature, for they have been transformed by an adopted style and by that "punto di fantasia" that enables the artist to create his own style. The artist does not mirror nature; rather, using nature as a point of departure, he imagines and creates something new, something in which style or form is also an expression of his personal *fantasia* and is, therefore, expressive of his personality or character.

Certainly Giambono drew from nature just as Cennini advised, for in some of his paintings are objects depicted with an uncommon accuracy of detail. In his signed *Madonna and Child* in Rome (plate 3), for example, the bird to the right, below the Christchild, seems to have been closely imitated from nature, although its undulating contour shows that nature has been transformed by the artist's manner. There is also a degree of naturalism in Giambono's human figures, for instance in the anatomy of Christ's torso in the *Man of Sorrows* at Padua (plate 4), but we sense here, as we do elsewhere, that the artist has drawn the figure from memory. His figures also give the impression that they have been created according to formulas, which the artist recalled and repeated with only slight variation throughout his artistic life. Thus, for instance, the head and face of the figure of Saint Michael in Giambono's polyptych of ca. 1455 at Venice (plate 5) looks very much like the head and face of the Archangel at I Tatti (plate 2). It might be said, then, that although Giambono, like other late-Gothic artists, probably studied nature at first hand, ultimately his style, like theirs, is based on formulas that were derived from the art of his contemporaries and predecessors, and the relatively limited naturalism he pursued was applied to those formulas, never integrated with them in any fundamental way. In short, Giambono did not attempt that comprehensive synthesis of manner and truth to nature that is the Renaissance style.

As Cennini advised, Giambono studied and imitated the best masters of his time, but contrary to the Florentine's advice he seems to have studied more than one. Here is not the place to undertake a lengthy discussion of Giambono's sources, but mention may be made of a few instances of his "borrowings" from other artists. For example, the melancholic expression of the figure of *Saint Michael* (plate 5) in the Saint James polyptych is similar to that of figures in earlier altarpieces, such as the one that is signed by Lorenzo Veneziano and dated 1371 (plate 6), and in the sculptural group of ca. 1395 on the iconostasis in the church of San Marco, Venice by Jacobello and Pierpaolo dalle Masegne (plate 7). Moreover, his use of richly patterned drapery parallels Lorenzo's use of the same device, just as the graceful, delicately curving lines of his forms find an echo in the figures by the dalle Masegne.

He was equally influenced by the art of his contemporaries, most notably Gentile da Fabriano and Pisanello early in his career, and later Jacopo Bellini and the team of Giovanni d'Alemagna and Antonio Vivarini. The anatomical features of the Virgin's face in Giambono's *Madonna and Child* at Bassano (plate 8), for example, are similar to those of Gentile's Virgin in a fragment of a larger work at I Tatti (plate 9) and are also very close to those of Jacopo Bellini's Virgin in his panel in the Louvre (plate 10).[11] Furthermore, the folds of the drapery falling over the Virgin's left arm in Giambono's panel (plate 8) are almost an exact duplicate of the cor-

---

[11] For further discussion of such artistic relations between Giambono and Jacopo Bellini, see Norman E. Land, "Jacopo Bellini's Lost *St. Michael* and a Possible Date for Pisanello," *Zeitschrift für Kunstgeschichte* 45 (1982): 282–6.

responding folds in the Virgin's drapery in Bellini's (plate 10), and the way in which Giambono employs small, gold-dots in the Virgin's mantle to give a relatively convincing illusion of three-dimensionality is similar to the way in which Bellini uses the same device in his painting. (We should note that Jacopo seems to have derived the practice from works by Gentile da Fabriano, but developed it as a device for the depiction of light and shadow on his own.) The Berenson figure (plate 2), which might reflect Bellini's lost *Saint Michael* of 1430, once in the church of San Michele in Padua, also bears a striking resemblance to Jacopo's archangel Gabriel in his *Annunciation to the Virgin*, at Brescia.[12] In these figures the treatment of the hair, the facial features, even the drapery are similar to one another. Still, there is a distinctive quality to Giambono's panels that separates them from those of Gentile and Jacopo, and that quality is the result of that "punto di fantasia," to use Cennini's phrase, which enabled Giambono to transform his borrowings into a style that is unmistakably his own.

Gentile offers his viewers highly wrought and richly embellished images, which, nevertheless, maintain a spiritual repose, images that are, so to speak, florid in their composure. The forms of Jacopo Bellini's panels are infused with a concentrated, intellectual energy, the kind of energy that sustained his near-obsession with linear perspective. Giambono, however, achieved a distinct and independent expression, one that at times is equal in intensity to that of the best of his contemporaries working in the same idiom. His figures, always pensive and melancholic, often gaze downward as if focusing on some object invisible to the viewer. At the same time, they appear also to concentrate on a thought or an emotion. These withdrawn and self-absorbed saints are the pictorial expression of the artist's inner vision — his sense of higher truth — a vision of a community of saints, in the broadest theological sense of that word, united by a kind of mystical love and longing (a *pothos*) for Christ and the Virgin.

Gesture and facial expression are important features of Giambono's art, but the essence of his vision — a melancholic, yearning love — is no less embodied in the forms of his paintings. In the Berenson *Saint Michael* (plate 2), for example, the rhythmical, slowly undulating curves of the archangel's dalmatic and the thin, trans-

---

12 For a convenient illustration of Bellini's work, see Liana Castelfranchi Vegas, *International Gothic Art In Italy*, trans. B. D. Phillips, revised by D. Talbot Rice (London, 1968), plate 53.

lucent veils of crimson paint with which it is represented unite to lend the image a luminous, shimmering, almost ethereal quality, like that of the facade of the Ca' d'Oro as it is reflected in the dark, endlessly undulating water of the Grand Canal, and the opaque and textured cerulean blue of the background is perfectly attuned to the rich crimson and deep old-gold of the dalmatic, creating a mellow, autumnal effect, as if the universe, having endured the oppressive heat of the summer sun, now enjoys the waning warmth of a brilliant, yet gentle day in October. As do virtually all of Giambono's authentic paintings, the *Saint Michael* also embodies that faint hint of decay and death, itself containing the promise of rebirth, present in even the most perfectly beautiful of late-blooming flowers.

The Berenson panel and the other paintings by Giambono that we have been discussing are examples of how the artist could enrich his *fantasia* through the study of nature and the works of the best masters and examples, too, of how his imagination could transform that which he took from others into a style distinctively his own. Giambono's art involves *fantasia* in another of the senses employed by Cennini, who says that the artist is free to use his imagination to combine parts of various images into a single whole. His well-known example is the combination of part of a horse and part of a man to create a centaur, although Cennini does not identify the hybrid as such. As far as we know and to our everlasting regret, Giambono never created a centaur, but he certainly did combine parts of various animals to create such monsters as the one at the feet of the Archangel in the Berenson panel (plate 2). The ferocious, growling head of that demon has a canine quality; its webbed wings are bat-like; its sleek, muscular body is feline; and its coiled tail, serpentine.

Furthermore, if we expand upon Cennini's definition of this kind of *fantasia* to include the novel combination of various images in a single picture, we shall discover a facet of Giambono's art that has largely escaped his critics.[13] In his haunting and deeply moving *Veil of Veronica* in Pavia (plate 11), for example, Giambono lends a novel significance to a traditional image by slightly tilting the head of Christ to one side and showing His eyes half-closed, as if He is dead or dying, both features that are found in

---

[13] For more discussion of the iconography of Giambono's works, see Norman E. Land, "Two Panels by Michele Giambono and Some Observations on St. Francis and the Man of Sorrows in Fifteenth-Century Venetian Painting," *Studies in Iconography* 6 (1980): 29–51.

traditional images of the Man of Sorrows (see plate 4 for example). Giambono, then, presents Christ both as the Holy Face miraculously imprinted on Veronica's cloth and as the Man of Sorrows and thereby enriches and deepens the traditional allusion of the Sudarium to the Passion. Another example of how Giambono used his *fantasia* to create iconographical novelty is the Berenson *Saint Michael* (plate 2). Although certainly not unique, the enthroned Archangel is rare in Venetian painting and mosaics and nowhere, to my knowledge, is he represented in association with the Man of Sorrows and a monstrance.

We should notice that Giambono was not the first nor the only Venetian painter to treat subject matter in a remarkably innovative manner. For example, Jacobello Alberegno, who died in 1397, and the anonymous trecento master responsible for the triptych representing the Madonna of Humility and the Man of Sorrows flanked by Saints James and Francis in the Gallerie dell'Accademia, Venice are noteworthy and important predecessors in this regard. Giambono's older contemporary, Jacobello del Fiore, also created novel images, particularly his large representation of Justice-Venice flanked by the Archangels Gabriel and Michael (plate 12) of 1421 in the Gallerie dell'Accademia, Venice.[14]

Among the works of the great artists of the first half of the fifteenth century who worked in the late-Gothic style, Giambono's jewel-like paintings shine with only a slightly lesser light, and, as we have suggested, at least part of his success lies in the realm of *fantasia*, but not in that of the naturalistic imitation of nature. His paintings succeed because they show forth a quality and an expression different from that of any other artist. His *fantasia* succeeded, too, in terms of iconographical innovation, for, like some of his trecento predecessors and like Giovanni Bellini, Giorgione and Titian after him, he created novel combinations of images suggestive of meaning never previously explored.

While on the subject of Giambono's artistic success, we should mention, too, if only in passing, that his achievement is due not only to his *fantasia*, as important as that is, but also to his evident

---

14 For illustrations of Alberegno's and the anonymous master's works, see Ridolfo Pallucchini, *La pittura veneziano del Trecento* (Venice and Rome, 1964): 209–10, 214; figs. 645–50, 656. For a discussion of the iconography of Jacobello del Fiore's *Justice-Venice*, see Staale Sinding-Larsen, *Christ in the Council Hall: Studies in the Religious Iconography of the Venetian Republic*, Acta ad Archaeologiam et Artium Historiam Pertinentia, V (Rome, 1974), 175.

delight in the decorative. This fundamentally decorative quality of his panels was noticed, it appears, by no less a critic than Walter Pater. Venetian painters preceding Giovanni Bellini and Carpaccio, Pater explained,

> seem never to have been so much as tempted to lose sight of the scope of their art in its strictness, or to forget that painting must be before all things decorative, a thing for the eye, a space of color on the wall, only more dexterously blent than the mark of its precious stone or the chance interchange of sun and shade upon it — this, to begin and end with; whatever higher matter of thought, or poetry, or religious reverie might play its part therein, between.[15]

But what, after all, is Giambono's place in the history of modern painting in Venice? It must be recognized that his art is devoid of the Renaissance admiration for the art of Antiquity. Moreover, he shows only occasional interest in verisimilitude and knew little or nothing of *colorito* or naturalistic coloring. Although he was heir to certain aspects of the richly decorative Veneto-Byzantine style as it was transformed by such artists as Lorenzo Veneziano, his art is preeminently Gothic: "the ogive of a hundred sumptuous church and palace facades then gracing the canals of Venice is reflected in the graceful, richly flowing curves of his figures."[16] Indeed, his panels must be seen as the last splendid efflorescence of the purely Gothic in Venetian painting. His expression, the particular character of his art, wherein lies his vitality, is Gothic too — that simple, yet elegant blending of a melancholic awareness of natural decay, a hope of rebirth, and a longing for Love and His Mother. But the inwardness of his figures, their dreamy, semi-conscious state, also prefigures the *sogno* of Giorgione and the giorgionesque, just as his *fantasia*, in terms of iconographical innovation and personal style, is prophetic of much in Venetian painting, and in literature and architecture as well, at the end of the century and beyond. We cannot claim, nor should we, that Giambono is the father of modern painting in Venice; Giovanni Bellini quite rightly holds that exalted position. Rather his distinction, from the point of view of his-

---

[15] Pater, *The Renaissance*, 110.

[16] Phillip Hendy, *European and American Paintings in the Isabella Stewart Gardner Museum* (Boston, 1974), 101.

tory, is that he was the first in whom the poetry of modern Venice, even if only partially, bestirred itself. In other words, he seems to have been the first to grasp that the "punto di fantasia" of which Cennini timidly speaks is really the powerful voice and guide of the individual imagination. And, although we have lately stressed what might be called the "corporate mentality" of La Serenissima, it is the individual imagination as inner voice and divine guide — an idea which, although instinctive, might have reached Venice from the Near East through Avicenna and Ibn 'Arabi — that the city built in the water has always nourished and rewarded.

3: Luce Aurea

ONE OF THE BEST KNOWN, most moving and, indeed, most beautiful of Giovanni Bellini's works is the *Saint Francis* in the Frick Collection, New York (plate 13), painted in or around the year 1485. In the painting, which at some unknown date was cut down along its top edge, the saint stands barefooted on rocky ground. Leaning backward slightly, he has turned to his right-hand side, away from the viewer and has lowered his arms seemingly to catch in his hands the light shining from the left. His mouth is open as if he is singing or praying, and he gazes intensely into the upper left-hand corner of the painting. Behind him is the mouth of a cave and in front of that is his cell, constructed from the trunks and branches of small trees and one, living grapevine. Inside the cell is a lectern, on which are a book, a skull, and a crucifix with a crown-of-thorns. A bell, almost hidden among the leaves of the grapevine, hangs above the lectern. His sandals and walking stick are also within the cell. In the lower left-hand corner is a *cartellino*, bearing the artist's name, and above that a spout, down which flows water from the rock. Above the water-spout is a laurel tree, its foliage illuminated from the front. In the middle-ground an ass and a heron stand on a grassy plateau which bears a dry, leafless tree. Beyond the plateau a lone shepherd tends his flock close to the bank of a river, and across the river is a walled city with outlying buildings and above them, on top of a hill, a castle touches the blue, cloud-swept sky. In the upper left-hand corner, just above the luminous, green laurel tree, light breaks through from behind the dark clouds.

Anyone who has even casually perused the literature on the *Saint Francis* knows already that a number of scholars have proposed many different, but more or less convincing explanations of its subject matter. The most widely known of these in that of Millard Meiss, who, following Bernard Berenson and others, argued that the painting represents Saint Francis's stigmatization, which event took place on Monte Alverna in 1224, just two years before the saint's death. Some art historians, such as John Steer, Giles Robertson and Jennifer M. Fletcher, have accepted Meiss's identification, but others have not.[1] A. Richard Turner, for instance, holds that Bellini has represented the saint singing his own "Song of Created Things," and Frederick Hartt thinks that the artist has shown "an ecstatic communion of St. Francis with God in Nature."[2] In addition, John V. Fleming has insisted that the painting does not now and never has represented the stigmatization and should be titled "St. Francis in the Desert," and, most recently, Rona Goffen holds that the artist reiterates "the theme of Christ's Passion, without representing the stigmatization itself."[3]

Inspite of the lack of consensus among scholars about the painting's subject matter and the denial that it is a depiction of the stigmatization, several elements clearly link it with conventional representations of that event. The cave behind the saint, for example, is found in Paolo Veneziano's panel of the stigmatization from the Santa Chiara altarpiece (plate 14) completed in 1358, and the mountain surrounding the saint in Michele Giambono's painting in the Cini Collection, Venice (plate 15) of around 1435 finds a parallel in Bellini's picture. The castle on the hill in the Frick painting may also be found in Giambono's panel, as may the depiction of the saint with an open mouth. Moreover, the way in which the figure in Bellini's painting turns to the left-hand side echoes the placement of the figures in both Paolo's and Giambono's panels, al-

---

[1] Millard Meiss, *Giovanni Bellini's Saint Francis in the Frick Collection* (New York, 1964) (first published as "Giovanni Bellini's *St. Francis,*" *Saggi e Memorie di storia dell'arte* 3 (1963): 11–30). See also idem, "Giovanni Bellini's 'St. Francis'," *Burlington Magazine* 107 (1966): 27 (a letter-to-the-editor in which the author clarifies certain portions of his argument); Berenson, *Venetian Painting in America*, 95–105; John Steer, book review in *Burlington Magazine* 107 (1965): 533–4; Giles Robertson, *Giovanni Bellini* (Oxford, 1968), 76–77; and Jennifer M. Fletcher, "The Provenance of Bellini's Frick 'St. Francis'," *Burlington Magazine* 114 (1972): 206–14.

[2] A. Richard Turner, *The Vision of Landscape in Renaissance Italy* (Princeton, 1966), 59–65; and Hartt, *Italian Renaissance Art*, 415. See also, *The Frick Collection: An Illustrated Catalogue* (New York, 1968), 2:203–9 (with further bibliography); and Alistair Smart, "The *Speculum Perfectionis* and Bellini's *St. Francis,*" *Apollo*, 97 (1973): 470–6.

[3] John V. Fleming, *From Bonaventure to Bellini: An Essay in Franciscan Exegesis* (Princeton, 1982), 28 (the author discusses Bellini's painting within the context of the Franciscan literary tradition rather than the tradition of visual representations of the subject); and Rona Goffen, *Giovanni Bellini* (New Haven and London, 1989), 111.

though in those works the saint is kneeling on the ground. And even the saint's unusual, arms-downward gesture has a precedent in Giambono's figure. Lastly, like the figures in previous depictions of the subject, Bellini's saint bears the stigmata in his hands and visible foot. These similarities suggest that Bellini did, indeed, represent the stigmatization. Missing from his depiction, however, are two conventional elements that would incontrovertibly identify it as a representation of that event — the seraph or seraph-Christ of the saint's vision and the lines connecting the wounds of the saint with those of the seraph, both of which elements are prominent in Paolo's and Giambono's panels (plates 14 and 15). As Meiss noted, it is improbable that the painting ever contained a seraph, even in the portion cut from its top edge, and we may add that there is no evidence that connecting lines were ever present in it.

Nevertheless, there is an object in the painting that may be understood as a symbol of the seraph seen by Saint Francis on Alverna — the green laurel tree in the upper left-hand corner. This tree, which is placed where we might expect the seraph to appear and in the direction of which the saint fixedly gazes, has been interpreted as a reference to Moses's burning bush, "in line with attempts of St. Francis' followers to depict him as a second Moses,"[4] but it also, as Colin Eisler has pointed out, alludes to Christ because the *laurus nobilis* was believed to be fireproof and, thus, like the wood of the Cross, "which kept mankind from the fires of damnation."[5] Furthermore, Christ identifies Himself and His Passion with, not specifically laurel trees, but green trees in general, when on His way to Golgotha, He says, "For if they do these things in the green tree, what shall be done in the dry" (Luke 23:31). This utterance is the source of a symbolism often used in quattrocento paintings of Christ. For instance, in Piero della Francesca's *Resurrection of Christ* at Sansepolcro there are green trees to the right and dry trees to the left.[6] And in Bellini's *Crucifixion* (now in the Palazzo Niccolini, Florence), painted around the same time as the *Saint Francis*, the Cross is flanked by dry trees, while off to the left-hand

[4] Hartt, *Italian Renaissance Art*, 415.

[5] Colin Eisler, "In Detail: Bellini's *Saint Francis*," *Portfolio* (April-May 1979): 21. See also Goffen, *Giovanni Bellini*, 111.

[6] Hartt, *Italian Renaissance Art*, 273 discusses tree symbolism in Piero's painting. See also Paul Barolsky, "Metaphorical Meaning in the Sistine Ceiling," *Source: Notes in the History of Art* 9 (1990): 19–22.

side is a green laurel that looks remarkably like the one in the Frick painting.[7] Similarly, in the *Saint Francis*, in addition to the green laurel tree, there is the dry tree behind the ass on the plateau in the middle-ground and another, smaller one between the saint and the ass. These trees together may allude to Christ's crucifixion and appropriately so, for the saint's stigmatization was understood by many to have been a "renewal" of that event.

According to literary sources available to Bellini, such as the *Considerazione sopra le sacre sante stimmate*, an appendix to the *Fioretti*, which was compiled in the fourteenth century from earlier sources, the saint's stigmaization was foretold in a vision that he experienced early during his stay on Alverna. While marveling at the deep fissures of the mountain, Saint Francis was told by God that they were made at the hour of Christ's Passion, and it was further revealed to him that the crucifixion would be renewed on Alverna, both in his body by means of the stigmata and in his soul through love and compassion.[8]

The significance of the green tree in Bellini's painting may also lie in its relation to the nature of the saint's vision. Tommaso da Celano in *The First Life* explains that in his vision Saint Francis saw "God as a man like a seraph, having six wings, with hands extended and feet joined together, affixed to a cross" ("Vidit in visione Dei virum unum, quasi Seraphim, sex alas habenten, stantem supra, manibus extensis, ac pedibus conjunctis, cruci affixum"), and in the *Legend of the Three Companions*, the saint's vision, now more complex, is described as "a seraph, within the wings of which was the form of a beautiful crucified man, having his hands and feet extended in the mode of a cross" ("apparuit ei Seraph unus, sex alas habens, et inter alas gerens formam pulcherrimi hominis

---

[7] For a color-reproduction of this painting, see Leonardo Ginori Lisci, *The Palazzi of Florence: Their History and Art*, trans. Jennifer Grillo (Florence, 1985), 1:221, fig. 183.

[8] *I Fioretti del glorioso messere Santo Francesco e de'suoi frati*, ed. Giovanni L. Passerini (Florence, 1919), 155. Passerini's edition is based upon a fifteenth-century manuscript in the Biblioteca Riccardiana, Florence (cod. 1670): "et allora fu revelato da Dio che quelle fessure cosi maravigliose erano state fatte miracolosamente, nell'ora della paxione di Christo, quando, secondo dice lo Evangelista, le pietre si sprezzarono. Et questo volle Idio che singularmente, aparisse in su quel monte della Vernia, a significare che in esso monte si doveva rinovare la paxione di Christo Jhesu nell'anima sua per amore e compaxione, e nel corpo per impressione della Stigmate."

crucifixi, manus quidem et pedes extensos habentis in modum crucis").[9] Saint Bonaventure is more explicit about the nature of the vision which he describes as "Christ under the species of Seraph" ("Christus sub specie Seraph").[10] Thus, according to the saint's biographers, the vision was at once both an angel and the crucified Christ.

In the Frick painting the green laurel tree, symbol of Christ and the Cross and the object of the Saint Francis's gaze, may be seen to stand in place of the saint's vision. In other words, Bellini seems to have symbolized the saint's vision of the seraph-Christ by means of the laurel tree illuminated by the light flooding the scene from the left, a light which appears to be, as we shall see, the artist's substitute for the lines conventionally employed to connect the wounds of the saint and his vision.

There has been much discussion about the source or sources of light in Bellini's painting. Meiss observed that the picture contains two kinds of light — one, an "unnatural" light, emanating from under the clouds in the upper left-hand corner, and the other, a "natural" light, shining from just outside the left-hand edge and a little in front of the picture's surface and illuminating the saint.[11] Other scholars, such as Turner and Robertson, see only one source of light in the painting, the sunlight shining from under the clouds in the upper left-hand corner, and Fleming, who thinks the saint "faces the rising sun," implies that there can be no "empirical certainty" about the nature and source or sources in the painting, that we are forced to fall back upon unverifiable observation.[12]

Nevertheless, we may observe that the light shining from under the clouds and falling upon the buildings in the distance is in such a position that it could not possibly illuminate the front of the laurel tree, nor create the saint's shadow, those of the wooden seat

[9] *Acta sanctorum*, October, II, 648. Cited by Millard Meiss, *Painting in Florence and Siena after the Black Death* (Princeton, 1951), 118 notes 48, 50.

[10] Meiss, *Painting in Florence and Siena*, 118.

[11] Meiss, *Giovanni Bellini's St. Francis*, 27.

[12] Turner, *Vision of Landscape*, 60; Robertson, *Giovanni Bellini*, 76–77; and Fleming, *From Bonaventure to Bellini*, 129. According to Fleming, "there is in pictorial analysis no more empirical certainty than there is in poetic analysis...I cannot, therefore, appeal, as I would wish to do, to the empirical fact that in this painting Francis of Assisi faces the rising sun..." See also Goffen, *Giovanni Bellini*, 110, who sees two kinds of light in the painting.

in his cell, or those of the hooves of the ass in the middle-ground. Certainly there are two sources of light, one shining from under the clouds and the other from outside the left-hand edge, just as Meiss observed. But a comparison of these lights with the light in other paintings of the stigmatization indicates that the one in the upper left-hand corner is sunlight, and the other is not a "natural" light, as Meiss thought, but a natural-looking light that is really supernatural in character.

In conventional representations of the saint's stigmatization, there are two different ways of depicting the lines connecting the seraph-Christ and the wounds in the saint's body. One way, exemplified in Giambono's panel (plate 15), was to color the lines red, which color appears to be an allusion to the blood of Christ, and, thus, perhaps to the physical likeness between Him and the saint. The other way of representing the connecting lines was to overlay them with gold-leaf, as in, for example, the panel by Paolo Veneziano from the Santa Chiara altarpiece (plate 14) and the *Stigmatization* by Domenico Veneziano from his Saint Lucy Altarpiece (plate 16). Because lines of gold-leaf are often used in trecento and quattrocento paintings to symbolize a supernatural illumination, or a divine presence, we may assume that in paintings like that of Domenico Veneziano they are signs of the "luce aurea" or golden light that, according to a number of sources, accompanied the appearance of the seraph-Christ on Alverna. The lines of gold in depictions of the stigmatization suggest, too, the spiritual similarity between Christ and Saint Francis.

In Domenico's painting (plate 16) there are two kinds of light, the natural light shining upon the landscape and figures and the supernatural light of the gold-lines uniting Saint Francis and his vision. Similarly, in Bellini's painting, there may be distinguished two kinds of light, the sunlight shining from the upper left-hand corner and the supernatural light emanating from the left-hand side and illuminating the foreground. Perhaps Bellini found the connecting lines in paintings like those of Giambono and Domenico too clumsy and too obstructive. In fact, in his own earlier version of the subject in the predella of the Pesaro *Coronation of the Virgin* (plate 17), he had gone a long way in eliminating them and in reducing the prominence usually given the seraph.

The influence of Netherlandish painting in fifteenth-century Italy, including Venice, is a well-known fact, and it may be no coincidence that Bellini's treatment of Saint Francis's stigmatization is foreshadowed in certain works by the Limbourg brothers and by Jan van Eyck.[13] For example, in an illumination in the *Belles Heures* (fol. 171) of the Duc de Berry, representing the stigmatization, there are no lines connecting the wounds of the vision with those of the saint, and the same is true of Jan van Eyck's painting in the Galleria Sabauda, Turin (plate 18). Moreover, in van Eyck's painting the size of the vision in relation to that of the saint is greatly reduced, just as in Bellini's Pesaro predella (plate 17).

Perhaps Bellini had seen a painting like van Eyck's before beginning his own version of the stigmatization in the Frick. In any case, by the time he came to paint that picture the connecting lines and even the supernatural vision would have seemed contrary to his desire for poetic realism. Thus, he discarded the golden lines of conventional representations and replaced them with a natural looking light, which by its position in the painting and its association with the laurel tree suggests that it is the divine light that appeared with the seraph-Christ on Alverna.

We have argued that the Frick *Saint Francis* is after all a representation of the stigmatization, although a dramatically innovative one in which Bellini has radically transformed the conventional depiction of the saint's vision of the seraph-Christ and its light. But the artist, as number of scholars have remarked, clearly does more than illustrate a single event. The importance of the landscape, for instance, reminds us, in the words of Johannes Wilde, that "Nature, as God's creation, was also the subject of contemplation to the Saint who preached to the birds and composed the Song of Brother Sun."[14] Indeed, the ecstatic mood of the painting; the animals and flowers; the laurel tree; the water flowing from rock; the saint's cell and the objects within — all these strongly suggest that the picture represents a kind of meditation upon the saint's stay on Alverna in relation to its theologically and historically most important event, the stigmatization and the simultaneous transformation of Saint

---

[13] For discussions of the Netherlandish influence on Italian art, see Millard Meiss, "Jan van Eyck and the Italian Renaissance," in *Venezia e l'Europa: Atti del XVIII congresso internazionale di storia dell'arte, 1955* (Venice, 1956), 58–69; and idem, "'Highlands' in the Lowlands: Jan van Eyck, the Master of Flémalle and the Franco-Italian Tradition," *Gazette des Beaux-Arts* 57 (1961): 273–314. Both articles are reprinted in idem, *The Painter's Choice: Problems in the Interpretation of Renaissance Art* (New York, 1976).

[14] Wilde, *Venetian Art*, 29.

Francis into "another Christ" or *alter Christus*.[15]

Nor should we forget that meaning in Bellini's painting may be expressed in its form as well as in its subject matter. The essentially nineteenth-century notion, recently modified by Fletcher and by Wilde, that the subject of the *Saint Francis* is merely Bellini's pretext for painting a landscape, no longer holds much authority. Still, the saint's surroundings are infused with a calm and moderate, yet deeply felt emotion, an emotion that stems from the artist's love of nature, and this emotion, religious in content, is certainly part of the meaning of the painting. And one cannot overlook the importance of the landscape as the setting for the saint's intense, yet restrained spiritual drama. There is in the composition of the landscape and its relation to the saint a sense of wholeness and completeness expressed not so much in harmonious form as in what might be called "a poetry of form," a visual rhyming of shapes. For instance, the shape of the small, circular dots of reflected light in the saint's eyes repeat the shape of the wounds in his hands and foot, as if to hint at a connection between the light into which he looks and the stigmata, and the shape of the skull under the crucifix on the lectern echoes the shape of his head, visually linking the crucifix and the stigmatized saint. On a larger scale, the upward movement of the saint's arms, broken at intervals by the folds of his habit, is repeated in the rocky contour of the mountain in the foreground as it slowly rises from the lower-left hand corner towards the opening of the cave and in the slope of the hill leading up to the castle in the distance. The movement of the saint's body as he leans backward slightly is repeated by the laurel tree as it rises at a parallel to the edge of the painting before gently curving inward, while the trunks of the two trees at the top of the painting above the saint curve in the opposite direction. These visual "rhymes" are not merely formal devices, for the composition seems to respond to the saint, specifically to the gesture of his arms and the movement of his torso, which, in turn, are the result of a dramatic action of his soul in response to the green laurel tree and to the light into which he looks.

The sheer beauty of Bellini's painting, so rich and resonant with meaning, convinces us that it represents his certainty about and knowledge of the significance of Saint Francis's stay on Alverna.

---

15 For Saint Francis as an *alter Christus* in Bellini's painting, see Land, "Two Panels by Michele Giambono," 29–41 (with further bibliography); and Fleming, *From Bonaventure to Bellini*, 140.

We sense this certainty and knowledge not only in the painting's invention, the way in which it is composed, but in its every aspect, and above all, perhaps, in its redolent *aria* and in the careful attention the artist has given to every detail. "One feels," as Turner has explained, "that the spiritually significant emanates from a simple love of objects observed. Through familiarity with things known the artist would join the spirit and the unknown."[16] We might even say that the subtle finish he gave to rock and tree, sky and flower expresses his own Franciscan love of nature.

"Pieno d'amore," Saint Francis, only a few moments ago seated and meditating upon the Passion of Christ, now stands, bare feet on holy ground, all transfigured with his back to his cell. Fervent and devoted bearer in peace and joy of life's "infirmities and trials," he waits patiently in this "place suitable for contemplation," at the exact center of the universe, as good Sister Earth, bathed in the dewy freshness of this morning of the Holy Cross, revolves around him. Leaning backward slightly, he humbly looks into the bright light. This light, "comely and joyful and vigorous and strong," is reflected in his compassionate eyes, creating in their pupils tiny, moist dots of illumination. Awaiting his eventual metamorphosis, the Poverello, "a most vile and abominable and contemptible worm," speaks into the "depths of the infinite goodness and wisdom and power" of the transforming light, as he stands on this Golgotha-like outcropping of hard, sharp rock, which puts "forth different fruits with colored flowers and grass" and provides habitation for one of God's humblest creatures, the hare staring out at the saint from its hole. Behind him, just outside the mouth of the cave, which could also serve as a tomb, is a shelter, or cell constructed of slender saplings, cut down and tied together, and of one, living grapevine.

> I am the true vine, and my Father is the husbandman. Every branch in me that beareth not fruit he taketh away: and every branch that beareth fruit, he purgeth it, that it may bring forth more fruit. Now ye are clean through the word which I have spoken unto you...I am the vine, ye are the branches: he that abideth in me, and I in him, the same bringeth forth much fruit: for without me ye can do nothing.

---

16 Turner, *Vision of Landscape*, 58.

On the lectern, at the foot of the thorn-ringed crucifix, the hollow-eyed skull, grim reminder of death, gazes in the same direction as the saint as he undergoes a spiritual demise and transformation. On the other side of the painting, above a deep fissure in the rock, one of the congregation of birds that showed joy at the saint's coming to Alverna sits on a barren branch bearing a *cartellino* carrying the artist's name, and just above it Sister Water, "useful and humble and rare and chaste," miraculously flows from a spout in the dry rock to quench a peasant's thirst. Emerging above this spring, a tall, slender laurel sapling seems all ablaze, like Moses's burning bush, not with fire, but with the golden, "fiery light" illuminating the saint. In the middle-ground, past the living rock surrounding the saint, a peasant's uncomprehending mule and a heron stand on a plateau covered with the greenest of new grass, and beyond them, on an even lower ground, a shepherd leans on his staff as he watches over his flock. Behind the shepherd, across the river with its bridge and dam, a walled city, perhaps Chiusi in Casentino, lies in the warm sunlight just below a hill on top of which the walls of a castle, perhaps that of Count Orlando, who invited the saint here, are silhouetted against the blue cloud-swept sky. In the far distance, azure mountains touch the heavens, and in the upper left-hand corner, from under the clouds, the glorious light of Brother Sun, "fair and radiant with a great shining," breaks through.

4: The Potted Tree

IN THE FOREGROUND of Giovanni Bellini's so-called *Sacred Allegory* in the Uffizi Galleries (plate 19) is a floor of inlaid red, black and white marble surrounded on three sides by a marble balustrade. The pattern in the floor is composed of a central square with narrow octagonal lozenges around its circumference. Two bands of alternating red and black marble intersect the center of the square, which is also the center of the floor. Here a fair-haired male infant firmly plants his feet in an urn holding a tree. The infant shakes the slender trunk of the tree causing large golden apples to fall from its branches while another nude male infant bends to pick up one of the fallen fruits. A third infant is clothed in a short, white tunic and is seated on a crimson cushion at the center of the panel. This clothed infant, contemplating the golden apple in his hands, is Christ.

To the right of the tree, beyond the infant who bends to pick up an apple, stand Saint Sebastian, his milk-white flesh pierced by two arrows, and behind him, a deeply tanned Job, who, like his companion, was especially revered by the Venetians. Job holds his hands in prayer or reverence as he meditates upon the tree, and one feels that Saint Sebastian, who gazes fixedly at the tree, would hold his hands as Job does, were they not tied behind him. On the other side of the floor, the Virgin is seated in a throne with a raised, marble base extending slightly into the square in the pavement. In the dark area on the base of the throne there is a barely visible relief of a reclining female figure. Mary holds her hands together before her and leans forward slightly as she gazes intensely at the tree and its urn.

Out of the back of the Virgin's throne rises a cornucopia-like support for the blood-red canopy above her. At the center of the canopy is a gold-ornament, like a covered chalice, below which are bunches of grapes, also of gold, hanging from the mouth of the horn. Flanking the Virgin on her left-hand side and turned towards her stands a young woman clothed in a blue mantle and red

tunic and crowned with a diadem. To the Virgin's right, exactly opposite Saint Sebastian, another young woman, her mouth open as
if she speaks, is clothed in a dark blue mantle and white tunic. She,
too, looks towards the tree as she floats, miraculously, above the
floor. Both of these young women, in imitation of the Virgin, hold
their hands in a gesture of prayerful reverence.

Just behind the tree and enframing it, the doors of a gate in the
center of the balustrade stand open. Outside the gate, Saint Peter in
a posture of prayer leans on the balustrade and turns his head towards the tree, while Saint Paul with one hand raises a sword, the
tip of which points towards the gold chalice on the summit of the
Virgin's sheltering canopy, and rests the other hand, holding a
scroll, on the balustrade. He faces toward our left-hand side, and his
mouth is open as if he speaks. Outside the gate, behind Peter and
Paul, a strip of nearly barren ground runs the width of the panel.
Leaves of dead grass cover this ground, and five dry and leafless
saplings stand at regular intervals along it. On the left-hand edge of
the panel, a man in a white turban walks slowly along the lifeless
strip of ground and out of the picture, perhaps driven by the words
of Paul and by his sword.

From the right-hand side of the panel, just beyond the sterile
ground, a mass of rock juts out into a lake. Along the near edge of
this promontory, sheep and goats lie down or wander about, while
their keeper, simply dressed in a red shirt and white trousers, sits
in a dark cave and rests his head on one hand. He seems to be lost
in some private musing as he gazes into the darkness of his cave,
envisioning, perhaps, his own *vita nuova*. Above the shepherd's
cave and to the right-hand side, a road leads into the panel and
ends at a wooden Cross. To the right of the Cross, a man, identifiable as Saint Anthony Abbot, slowly descends a stairway that
connects the plateau above and the rocky banks of the lake below.
There, on the edge of the lake, a centaur — perhaps the good centaur Chiron, sagacious teacher of gods and goddesses — awaits the
saint, who slowly descends the stairs.

On the other side of the painting, another mass of rock, this one
uninhabited, rises out of the water, and on the far side of the lake,
at the foot of a mountain of sheer rock, a village lies in the warm
sunlight. In front of the village a man with a stick over his shoulder walks into the sun, as does another man driving a mule. To the
left two figures, each as white as Istrian stone, embrace one another
as they stand as still as statues in a public square. Behind the village

rises a tree-covered hill at the top of which is a castle silhouetted against the blue, cloud-swept sky.

Since the beginning of this century, many scholars have attempted to explain the meaning of the subject matter of Bellini's painting. First, Gustav Ludwig proposed that Bellini has here illustrated a mystical, French poem of the fourteenth century by Guillaume de Guilleville in which a pilgrim dreams that he and an angel travel through Hell, Purgatory and Paradise.[1] Ludwig's interpretation remained unchallenged until Niccolò Rasmo pointed out certain inconsistencies in it.[2] Rasmo, furthermore, identified the figure leaning on the balustrade as Joseph, not Peter, and thought that the subject matter of the painting is the Holy Family. A few years later Philippe Verdier, following the lead of Ludwig, identified the subject matter as a sacred allegory and explained its meaning with reference to certain medieval commentaries on Psalm 84.[3] Wolfgang Braunfels, finding Verdier's explanation overly complex, suggested that the area in the foreground is a Paradise-garden.[4] Susan Delaney has recently explained that the small tree in the urn at the center of the floor is a Charity Tree. She also argues that the unifying theme of the various iconographical elements is "their relationship to the Church."[5] Marco Lattanzi and Stefano Cotellacci, expanding upon Delaney's interpretation, identified the tree in the foreground as the Tree of Life and suggested that the theme of the painting is the attainment of paradise through the *vita contemplativa*, and Rona Goffen, too, has stressed the meditative mood of the painting: "Perhaps allegory is an inappropriate characterization of the scene, which might better be

---

[1] Gustav Ludwig, "Giovanni Bellini's sogenannte Madonna am see in den Uffizien: eine religiose Allegorie," *Jahrbuch der Königlich Preussischen Kunstsammlungen* 23 (1902): 163–86.

[2] Niccolò Rasmo, "La sacra conversazione belliniana degli Uffizi e il problema della sua comprensione," *Carro minore* 5–6 (1946): 229–40.

[3] Philippe Verdier, "L'Allegoria della Misericordia e della Giustizia di Giambellino agli Uffizi," *Atti dell'istituto veneto di scienza, lettere ed arti* 109 (1952–1953): 97–116.

[4] Wolfgang Braunfels, "Giovanni Bellini's Paradiesgärtlein," *Das Munster* 9 (1956): 1–13.

[5] Susan J. Delaney, "The Iconography of Giovanni Bellini's *Sacred Allegory*," *Art Bulletin* 59, (1977): 331–5.

described as a 'meditation on the Passion'."[6]

All of the above-mentioned scholars, to one extent or another, have contributed to and enhanced our understanding of the iconography of Bellini's painting. (Indeed, some elements of my own interpretation of the subject matter are drawn from their studies.) Still, those scholars have also, I think, done the painting something of a disservice, for they have, in effect, reduced it, just as others have reduced Giorgione's *Tempest* (plate 1), to a mere problem for iconographers. They have largely overlooked those qualities that accompany the subject matter and give to it a meaning other than textual. In other words, while searching for texts and images that will help us to understand the subject matter of Bellini's painting, art historians have largely ignored the painting's form and its particular beauty. Likewise, they have given little attention to the meaning of the form or to the relation between form and subject.

As has been mentioned already, the floor in the foreground of Bellini's painting has a balustrade on three sides. The fourth side, however, although not visible, is implied. It extends along the bottom of the panel just out of sight. The painting thus suggests that we, like Peter opposite us, stand behind a balustrade, and as we do so, we gaze upon the tree, which stands at the center of the perspective. Moreover, the painting invites us to assume, if not outwardly at least inwardly, the gesture and attitude of Saint Peter, Job, the Virgin, and her companions. And in such an attitude we realize that the painting requires us to meditate upon this unfamiliar place of holy mystery and its inhabitants.

The tree with its golden fruit at the center of the floor makes us recall the Tree of Life, but also, and at the same time, the Tree of the Knowledge of Good and Evil. Here, in this place of marble and geometry, original sin is conquered in a moment: the old Eden and the old tree have been transformed into this new paradise and the Tree of Eternal Life. The tree, then, gives meaning to Job, who may be seen as a kind of Old Testament proto-martyr, and to Saint Sebastian, who died for his beliefs. Their physical pain and spiritual submission are means to vision of the tree, which they now see "with their own eyes." Similarly, the Virgin and the infant Christ

---

[6] Marco Lattanzi and Stefano Cotellacci, "Studi belliniani: proposte iconologiche per la Sacra allegoria degli Uffizi," in *Giorgione e la cultura veneta tra '400 e '500: mito, allegoria, analisi iconologica* (Rome, 1981), 59–79; and Goffen, *Giovanni Bellini*, 111.

make us remember the Incarnation, and the tree and the urn together thus become an emblem of that miraculous birth, one of the events that make possible this terrestrial paradise. The other event, of course, is the Crucifixion, which is reflected in the sufferings of Job and Saint Sebastian, as well as in the slaughter of the *innocenti*, which event we also recall, and is symbolized by the chalice and by the grapes under the Virgin's canopy, itself bearing a golden cross. The tree in the center of the floor and Christ in the center of the panel are together one center or two different centers of one circle, and the tree is Adam's old tree, but also the tree from which the Cross was fashioned. We should remember, too, in this connection that on his way to Golgotha, Christ referred to Himself as "the green tree": "If they do this in the green tree, what shall they do in the dry? (Luke 23:31)."

Birth, Death and the New Life: these are the great themes suggested in the foreground of Bellini's painting. A somewhat lesser theme is also implied. Outside the gate in the balustrade Peter and Paul, who stand among the dry trees, remind us of the Church and by implication suggest to us that this paradise is, as it were, a kind of *chiesa al fresco*. Indeed, the foreground implies a meaning similar to that of Raphael's *Disputà*. The Church is not merely a building or a collection of petrified dogmas; the Church is the supple, green tree and those holy mysteries for which it stands — birth, death and eternal life. The painting further suggests that this paradise, which is also Mother Church, is continuous with all of nature. We might even say that in this painting the holy mysteries of birth, death and resurrection are seen to underlie the natural cycles of all life.

Iconographical meaning in Bellini's painting is rich, elusive and inexhaustible, but meaning is not confined to subject matter; it is also an expression of form and content. Even the longitudinal rectangle of the support, for example, evokes the spiritual repose of the saints gathered here in the foreground around this deceptively small tree. And the opalescent lake, without ripple or wave, reflecting the rocks, the sky and the clouds in the sky, lies calm to its darkest depths. The great masses of rock rising from the water on either side of the painting lend it a sense of monumental stability, and the mountain in the background reaching upward to the heavens conveys a sense of self-possession and timeless quiet reminiscent of the Eugenean hills seen from Venice on a clear day. The mood of pristine serenity is enhanced by the sunlight which bathes the landscape and foreground alike in a fresh warmth like that of a morning in early June. Moisture rising from the lake saturates the light-filled air, which seems to envelop and to caress the human figures and to soften the sharp edges of the rocks. This lucent atmosphere unites all objects in such a way that nothing has the air of isolation and nothing intrudes upon the pervasive calm. There is no music here, either. No rhythm divides this stillness, nor underlies this repose. Motion is confined to the *innocenti*, who move with disarming confidence around the double still-points of Christ and the green tree, and to the periphery, where the men walk along the far shore, the saint quietly descends the stairs, and the infidel walks slowly, but deliberately out of the picture. But this slow deliberate movement, ever approaching a focussed stillness, serves only to enhance the columnar verticality of the motionless saints, whose spiritual serenity finds its sensuous analogues in the light and in the landscape behind them.

In the foreground, the long horizontal and short vertical shapes of the marble floor and the balustrade echo the shape of the support and anchor the painting to its edges. These forms are further echoed in the background, especially in the buildings in the distant village and the castle on the hill, but also in the entrance to the shepherd's cave and in the wooden Cross at the end of the road to the right in the middle-distance. As we look more closely, we see that nature itself seems to partake of a geometrical perfection. Where the water meets the rocky promontories, there are irregular horizontals, and the corner of the rock just behind the centaur is almost a true perpendicular. The verticality of the mountain in the background and the lateral extension of the horizon also suggest geometry. But even in the foreground all is not horizontals and verticals. There are also the soft curve of the body of the infant, who bends to pick up an apple, and the gentle roundness of Christ's back as he leans forward to contemplate the apple in his hands, as well as the delicate curve of the Virgin's shoulders as she leans ever so slightly towards the green tree. These small curvilinear shapes in the foreground are repeated in the clouds as they are blown across the cerulean sky and, on a much broader scale, in the rocky projections of the middle-ground as they move slowly from either side downward into the tranquil depths of the dark green lake.

Of course, many Renaissance paintings are composed of horizontals, verticals and curves, but in this painting much of Bellini's poetry is conveyed through those common elements. It might be said, borrowing a line from Charles Williams, that in this painting "curves of golden life define the straitness of a perfect line." The geometrical perfection of the foreground is enhanced and made significant by the "curves of golden life" within its confines. Likewise, in the background, the curves of nature gain a kind of meaningful presence for the landscape from the contrast with the straitness of perfect lines. The mutual enhancement of curve and straight line is also at work in a larger way, for the rectilinear geometry of the foreground with its lesser curves is a reversed image of organic nature with its lesser geometry. Gradually, we are convinced that in Bellini's vision the terrestrial paradise and nature are opposite poles of a continuum, each defining and lending meaning to the other. But this is not the whole of the painting's poetry, for there is also the sense that the continuum "thinks itself" in Bellini and that he is its "consciousness."

Several authors, including Verdier, Norbert Huse and Egon Verheyen, have linked Bellini's painting to a *fantasia* or *poesia* Bellini said he would paint for Isabella d'Este, but probably never did.[7] Although the association of the panel with Isabella's commission is seemingly incorrect, it nevertheless points to one of the painting's salient qualities. Bellini once told Pietro Bembo that he did not like to have many written instructions about subject matter when he painted a picture. Rather, as he said, he "always liked to wander at will in his paintings" ("sempre vagare a sua voglia nelle pitture").[8] In this picture the unfamiliar foreground and its conjunction with familiar nature suggest that we are contemplating a *fantasia*, the product of a mind wandering freely at will. But the foreground, however unfamiliar and fantastic, is not shocking or jarring, nor does it look out of place. It seems to be of a piece with nature, and we sense no incongruity between paradise and nature, for the foreground is not mystical in the sense that it does not carry us to some abstraction outside of what we see.

The foreground and its inhabitants and the landscape with its

---

[7] Verdier, "L'Allegoria della Misericordia," 115; Egon Verheyen, *The Paintings in the 'Studiolo' of Isabella d'Este at Mantua* (New York, 1971), 16; and Norbert Huse, *Studien zu Giovanni Bellini* (Berlin and New York, 1972), 82–86.

[8] Giovanni Gaye and Alfred von Reumont, eds., *Carteggio inedito d'artisti dei secoli XIV. XV. XVI.*, 3 vols. (Florence, 1840), 2:71.

figures embody the same poetic reality, and that poetic reality has to
do with Bellini's vision of nature in which the divine is emanates
and informs all things, even the strip of barren ground just outside
the gate. Bellini makes us see that the world perceived through the
senses and the world of imagination are very different aspects of
the same reality, the *anima mundi*, or world soul. He makes us see
that imagination and physical reality intersect one another.

Bellini, then, as in his *Saint Francis* (plate 13), shows forth his
fantasia as it wandered round and about his subject matter, and we
have the distinct impression, too, that his fantasy wandered as he
discovered the form of his subject matter. Like the men who walk
on the far shore, Bellini wandered past the crisp, Italian village
rising from the water, up the steep road behind the buildings and
climbed the forbidding rocks so that he might gaze upon the sea in
the distance and watch the ships sailing slowly to the East until
they vanished over the horizon. And retracing his steps, he wandered along that other road and stood before the green tree, cut
down and fashioned into another thing. He wandered past the old
saint slowly descending the stairs, past the centaur, and peered for a
moment into the shepherd's cave. Then, finding himself on the
lifeless shore, he marveled at the five withered saplings and stood
between Peter and Paul to see the green tree in its urn, the inno-
cents, and Mary, enthroned and silhouetted against the clear, blue
water, reflecting rock, cloud, and sky.

Standing there in contemplation, he heard behind him the soft
lapping, lapping of water against the dry shore, a sound such as one
hears, when the Lagoon is calm, along the Molo, the easy lapping
and lapping of water against stone. This is the sound he would
have heard as he wandered at will in his painting. That sound, and
he would have heard the song of the *gondoliere*, the wondrous
clanging of bells marking the hour, the infinite voice of his com-
patriots talking through it all, above it all, the cry of seagulls, and
the creaking of wood against wood as ships rocked in the Bacino.
And he would have smelled as he wandered at will, the salty air of
the Adriatic breeze, the stench at low tide, bread baking, strong
vino tocai, the blue smoke of incense burning in dark churches,
fish and eel, ripe fruit at the Rialto, and more. He would have
touched the smooth marble, the rough stone, bricks and moist stuc-
co, and the oily skin of African oranges.

We, too, hear in the moment of Bellini's painting the gentle
rustling and shifting of leaves as the nude, innocent children play

around the green tree, and we hear the softly whispered prayers of the women. We hear, echoing from across the placid water, the clopping hooves of the centaur, and the slow, plodding feet of Saint Anthony as he quietly descends, forever descends, the stairs. We hear from the farthest shore the faint, small sound of the man walking with a staff over his shoulder, and, echoing through the rocks, the shout of the man driving the mule. In the distance, wind sweeps the clouds across the sky and roars around the corners of the castle on the hill. We hear the wind. But above all we hear the silence, the translucent silence that "peach-blossom marble speaks and basalt, antique black." It is the aqueous silence floating up from the deep, the dark green silence emanating from the depths of water. It is the cool silence of caverns reaching into the earth; the damp, dark, fragrant silence drifting up from the center of the earth. But it is also the warm, clear silence of the morning light of a day in early June.

John Ruskin believed that Bellini grew up in Venice at a time when religion was still imaginative, and therefore vital, before it had become merely formal, and the great critic therewith implied the unself-conscious vitality of religion in Bellini's art. Bernard Berenson also remarked the profound expression of religious emotion in the artist's paintings. Roger Fry, who acknowledged Bellini's religious feeling, nevertheless chose to stress a somewhat different quality of his art, the artist's love of sensuous beauty, which the critic appropriately compared to a Wordsworthian love of nature. Fry also underscored the element of "fancy" in Bellini's art, an element that is undeniably an indispensable part of the artist's poetic expression. Indeed, Bellini's world, as Frederick Hartt, echoing Walter Pater, pointed out, "is not accessible to analysis throughout and cannot always be rationally stated."[9] For Bellini, as for the viewer of his paintings, the truths of religion and nature "must be contemplated in conjunction with, not at the expense of, phantasy."[10]

As the great critics have taught us to see, Bellini's fundamental qualities are religious emotion, the truths of nature, and poetic

[9] Hartt, *Italian Renaissance Art*, 409. See also Pater, *The Renaissance*, 108, who says that meaning in Venetian paintings often "reaches us through ways not distinctly traceable by the understanding."

[10] Adrian Stokes, "Painting, Giorgione and Barbaro," *Criterion* 9 (1929–30): 493–4.

fantasy. But these qualities are not discrete components in his art. They are inextricably bound one to another, as in the painting in the Uffizi (plate 19), where "contemplation as a state of spirit and silence as the fertile condition which brings it forth are the subject."[11] Moreover, the painting seems to live "in the moment of beginning, in the mathematical exactitude of beginning," revealed to us in an ever-expanding moment of vision. And this pristine "moment of beginning" speaks both of the reality of spirit and of the reality of nature, which are in the artist's eyes, and in our own as we gaze upon the painting, continuous and inseparable. But Bellini's imagination does not impose the reality of the green tree upon nature. On the contrary, he draws nature to himself so that he may reveal reality in its fullness. Nor does he accent or insist upon the reality here revealed, as did some artists of the Renaissance. Without the slightest hint of self-consciousness, he puts squarely before us his vision of a transubstantiated nature, "of a divine order both informing and transcending nature,"[12] a vision of nature that is simultaneously as sensuous and concrete as human flesh and as spiritually and poetically present as the human soul.

[11] Turner, *Vision of Landscape*, 76–77.

[12] David Piper, *Looking at Art* (New York, 1984), 72.

5: La Serenissima

OFTEN THE RENAISSANCE is viewed as an era of intellectual illumination, of reason and a new consciousness, of mathematics and the scientific study of nature, but there is a quality in early sixteenth-century Venetian paintings, especially those of Giorgione (see Plate 1) and his followers, referred to as *sogno* or *sognonismo*, a dream-like atmosphere, which affirms other dimensions of human experience. The figures in Giorgione's Castelfranco altarpiece, for example, "bespeak withdrawal, as if their spirit were preoccupied by a remembered dream."[1] Not only are semiconscious states of mind prevalent in this art, sleep is a popular subject in paintings of the time.[2] Among other numerous works, a sleeping figure appears in Cima da Conegliano's *Endymion Asleep* in the Galleria Nazionale, Parma and in Lorenzo Lotto's so-called *A Maiden's Dream* in the National Gallery of Art, Washington (plate 20). Actually Lotto's figure is not dormant; rather, her drooping eyelids suggest that she is suspended in that luxurious, though sometimes terrifying, spiritual realm that lies between sleep and wakefulness.

In 1505, the year in or around which Lotto made his picture, having left his native city of Venice for reasons unknown, he was settled in Treviso. His painting is thought to have been originally designed as a cover for a now-lost portrait, just as his *Allegory of Vice and Virtue*, also in Washington, is thought to be the cover of his portrait of Bishop Bernardo de' Rossi in Naples.[3] *A Maiden's Dream* has been interpreted as an allegory of vice, personified by

[1] Sydney J. Freedberg, *Painting in Italy, 1500-1600*, The Pelican History of Art (Baltimore, 1975), 127.

[2] For this subject, see Millard Meiss, "Sleep in Venice: Ancients Myths and Renaissance Proclivities," *Proceedings of the American Philosophical Society* 110 (1966): 348–86 (reprinted in idem, *The Painter's Choice*, 212–39).

[3] More information about these two paintings may be found in Fern R. Shapley, *Paintings from the Samuel H. Kress Collection: Italian Schools XV-XVI*, 2 vols. (London, 1968), 2:158.

the satyrs in the lower portion of the painting, and of virtue, symbolized by the flowers dropped on the woman from above by an *amorino*.[4] In other words, the young woman is slowly being awakened from dark sensuality by a higher love, a love that bestows virtue upon her. *A Maiden's Dream* might be understood, then, as the expression of the particular *virtù* of a Renaissance man of distinction, a humanist perhaps, or one of humanist inclinations, or, if a woman, as the expression of the character of some reincarnation of Dante's Beatrice or Petrarch's Laura. Thus, the painting, which may be thought of as a kind of portrait, might have revealed, as it were, the very soul of the person whose visage it concealed, a "face" that would have prepared the viewer for the face he or she would meet in the portrait proper.

A similar allegorical theme runs through the *Hypnerotomachia Poliphili* (Venice, 1499) of Francesco Colonna, a Venetian friar and contemporary of Lotto.[5] The subtitle of this beguiling tale, known in English as *The Strife of Love in a Dream*, proclaims that all of human life is but a dream. Actually a dream-within-a-dream, the story tells of Poliphilo's stirring passions for Polia, and how those passions are purified and tamed by the rituals and trials he undergoes in pursuit of his beloved. The parallel between the theme of Lotto's painting and that of Colonna's book is interesting, but mentioned is made of it here for another reason as well. Intense contemplation of the painting will transform the viewers, if they are willing, into a Poliphilo, so that afterward they, like Colonna's hero, may lose themselves in reverie to love more completely.

Although Lotto's painting does, indeed, appear to be allegorical, it is also an excellent example of one of two kinds of imagination operative in Renaissance art, first described, as far as I know, by Violet Paget, who wrote under the pseudonym of Vernon Lee. One kind, she explained,

> is the imagination of how an event would have looked, the power of understanding and showing how an action would

---

[4] Guy de Tervarent, *Attributs et symboles dans l'art profane, 1450-1600*, 2 vols. (Geneva, 1959), 2:390–391.

[5] For a comprehensive bibliography on Colonna and his book, see Maria Teresa Casella and Giovanni Pozzi, *Francesco Colonna: biografia e opere*, 2 vols. (Padua, 1959), 1:xvii–xxxvii, and Giovanni Pozzi and Lucia A. Ciapponi, eds., *Hypnerotomachia Poliphili*, 2 vols. (Padua, 1964), 2:47–51.

have taken place, and how that action would have affected the bystanders; a sort of second-sight, occasionally rising to the point not merely of revealing the material aspect of things and people, but the emotional value of the event in the eyes of the painter.

One thinks here of Giotto, Leonardo da Vinci and Raphael. The other kind of imagination, that which is embodied, according to Paget, in the art of Fra Angelico, Benozzo Gozzoli, Botticelli, and "all those Venetians who painted piping shepherds, and ruralising magnificent ladies absorbed in daydreams," is the imagination

> which delights the mind by holding before it some charming or uncommon object, and conjuring up therewith a whole train of feeling and fancy; the school, we might call it, of intellectual decoration, of arabesques of forms not of lines and colours, but of associations, and suggests to us trains of thoughts and feelings unknown to the artist.[6]

Beyond doubt, Lotto's painting falls squarely into this second category of imaginative depiction. This circumstance leads us to the possibility that we may well be far from the truth when we think of Lotto's painting and others like it (e.g., Giovanni Bellini's so-called *Sacred Allegory;* plate 19) as allegories, at least insofar as allegories refer to such abstractions as Vice and Virtue. *A Maiden's Dream* is also an embodiment or manifestation of certain qualities and the presentation of certain presences. The picture, in other words, is both physical and imaginal, but unlike allegory, it is a reality that is both physical and imaginal at once: meaning, in the broadest possible sense, is inseparable from the form in which it is expressed.

Perhaps it is the water, languidly flowing beside the tender woman; or perhaps it is the *amorino* suspended, like a thought in the mind, in the cool, morning air; or perhaps it is that the painting stirs in us memory of Venice, effecting the sensation of drifting in a gondola, as if the artist himself, newly arrived in Treviso, invested his panel with the recollection of water contemplated in reveries — whatever the cause, we are convinced that "dreaming even in

---

6 Violet Paget [Vernon Lee, pseud.], "The Imaginative Art of the Renaissance," in *Renaissance Fancies and Studies* (New York and London, 1896), 69–70. The author's definition of this second category of imagination recalls Pater (*The Renaissance*, 108).

daytime might come to much" here. In other words, Lotto's painting, by whatever mysterious means, does, indeed, as Paget says, conjure in its viewers "a whole train of feeling and fancy...unknown to the artist," and if we would but allow ourselves the kind of freedom necessary to follow this fancy or "phantasy," we would draw nearer to the heart of the painting's meaning and significance than we would by employing purely rational means.

In the center of Lotto's enchanted landscape (plate 20), bathed in the light and atmosphere of breaking day, a young woman languidly reclines while an alertly attentive *amorino* gently sprinkles flowers over her from above. To the left, with an expression that mixes curiosity and caution, a female satyr peers out at her from behind a tree, and to the right a seated male satyr drunkenly holds a jug. Somewhere beyond the dark mountains in the distance, we might imagine, there lies a city of tall buildings, so tall that little sunlight reaches the streets below. There we find another artist, not Lotto himself, but some heir and kindred spirit — a wanderer, a pilgrim, a Poliphilo of sorts.

This Poliphilo looks about but can find no living being, neither man, woman, nor child, neither beast nor fowl. Presently, growing fearful and cold, for it is a cold place indeed, he wanders aimlessly and with growing apprehension in the dark maze for what seems an eternity, until at last he happens upon a man. This man's clothing suggests that he might be some kind of businessman, an insurance salesman perhaps, or a banker, but Poliphilo cannot make this out for certain. In any case, the man greets him politely and seems to have expected his arrival. The pilgrim asks him how he might find his way out of the dark and forbidding city, and the man replies that it is his mission to lead the lost soul out. Our hero wants to know about the man and about this dingy, uninhabited place, but the latter begins to walk away before Poliphilo can do so and presently beckons him to follow. At length, after so many turns that Poliphilo thinks he must be walking in a circle, the two figures come to the edge of the city, and the pilgrim, shivering and exhausted, beholds a flat strip of lush, green, well-kept grass, which leads to a dark woods in the distance.

Directly in front of Poliphilo, near the woods, is a building of modest size constructed in a style reminiscent of that of Palladio. The structure comprises two storeys united by gigantic pilasters of the Corinthian order and in each storey are large pedimented windows. On the facade, there are five windows above, and below, the central window is replaced by a pedimented door, which projects slightly away from the surface of the building and is framed by two half-columns. On either side of the entrance and in front of each pilaster is a large urn containing a laurel tree. These potted laurels seem to be placed around the entire structure. Entering the building, Poliphilo and his companion find themselves in a kind of antechamber lined with dark and polished mahogany. On the far wall of this chamber is a doorway, flanked by stairs leading up to the second floor. They pass through the doorway into a library, which contains books lining its walls and a large table with chairs in the center.

Silently retracing their steps and ascending the stairs to the second floor, they stand in a picture gallery containing nine relatively large paintings on canvas, four on each of the side walls and one on the end wall opposite the doorway. The pictures are arranged in this manner. On the west wall are paintings of 1.) a dark, dismal swamp, 2.) a mountain range like the Eugenean Hills, 3.) the city in which Poliphilo finds himself, and 4.) a river flowing through a pine forest. On the north wall is a portrait of Marsilio Ficino by Benozzo Gozzoli. On the east wall are pictures of 1.) a beach scene showing five dolphins leaping from a clear, blue ocean, 2.) a comfortable house in which resides an elegantly beautiful woman, 3.) a circular garden with a flower border of unending variety and an ancient oak tree in the middle, and 4.) an ancient burial cave.

In a matter-of-fact tone of voice the man offers Poliphilo a singular choice. He may, the stranger says, stay here and live in this building, or he may follow his guide into the woods in search of what he calls "the still-point." Poliphilo's senses are exhausted; he is weary and confused and wants desperately to remain in this dwelling and the comfort it seems to offer, but, even though he feels that the search for some vague, undefined "still-point" is foolish, there is a quality in his guide that leads the pilgrim to say that he will follow him into the woods, and leaving the building, the two set out towards the trees.

Almost immediately Poliphilo begins to regret his decision, for night, which has begun to fall, now compounds the darkness of the forest. Adding to the pilgrim's dismay, his companion speaks very little, as he walks steadily along the path he has found. He does pause from time to time to allow Poliphilo to catch him up and to inquire about his ability to go on, but other than on these occasions, the two walk in silence. After a long while, however, the man asks

Poliphilo if he knows the poetry of Dante, and the pilgrim responds that he has read portions of *Inferno*. This seems to displease his guide, who begins to speak at length of the poet, explaining intricacies of thought and allusion in the *Divina commedia* that poor Poliphilo finds difficult to grasp. Thus occupied, the companions walk through the forest for many miles until Poliphilo notices that he can just make out the light of day breaking through the trees ahead. Soon they emerge from the woods into a clearing or *launde* to behold a scene of unusual beauty and serenity.

Just above the mountains in the distance, the dark blue sky turns to streaks of pink and orange as the sun begins to rise and shed its light upon the leaves of the trees near by, lending them delicacy and animation, though there is no wind here, not even a breeze. Just to Poliphilo's left, from behind a tree peers a female satyr, her breasts bare. She calls softly to her male companion lying with his cloven feet stretched out in the grass to Poliphilo's right. Apparently he is oblivious to her summons, for his back is turned to her as he pours wine from a jug into his mouth. Between the two satyrs and further back at the center of the clearing is a most beautiful woman also lying on the ground with her back resting lightly upon the stump of a tree. A single branch grows up behind her from the stump, and beside her is a pool of clear water formed by a stream, the source of which Poliphilo cannot discern. Above the woman, illuminated by the soft light of the rising sun, hovers an infant with wings that move effortlessly as he drops the tiny blossoms of some modest flower upon her. He wears only a kind of apron filled to overflowing with these blossoms and floats on a cloud of them. The woman, whose head rests in one hand as if she has been napping, now fully awakens as Poliphilo and his guide draw nearer to her, and as she raises herself from the ground and approaches them, the pilgrim's companion whispers that he must leave him now and return to the city.

Poliphilo has grown fond of his guide and wants to follow him, but the woman's presence holds him fast, and as he turns towards her, he sees that she has long, light brown hair and wears a dress or tunic of the purest white. Thrown over her shoulders is a mantle of brilliant gold which sparkles in the increasing light as she stands before him. "Come," she says, "you must be thirsty," as she leads him by the hand to the pool of water. She draws a crystal globe, inside of which is a red rose, and a golden, ruby-studded chalice from behind the stump, and placing the globe in the water, she fills the chalice from the pool and gives it to him. No drink of water, or sweet wine, has ever tasted so good to him. It is cool and pure; it is living water, one might say. Refreshed, Poliphilo turns to the lady of the woods and thanks her. She, sensing his desire to ask about her and this place in which she dwells, says, "First, sleep. Then, all shall be revealed to you." He relishes the touch of the thick, soft grass as he follows her instructions and reclines.

Soon fast asleep, he dreams of an beautiful woman seated before him in a small boat. At first, he is entranced by her thick, auburn hair, the color of the heart of cedar-wood, falling in cascades upon her milk-white and befreckled shoulders. She wears a long white silk dress, tinged with green and embroidered with small, silver flowers. Her green eyes radiate bliss; her nose is straight and fine; her slender lips remind him of soft rose-petals. She so fills him with her beauty that for a long while he is content to gaze only upon her radiant face. Then, freeing himself from this intoxication, he asks, "Who are you and to where do you take me?" She replies in a gentle and peaceful voice, "I am a poet of the city, and your destination is that place to which you move."

Understanding somehow that the poet will explain matters no further, Poliphilo surveys the scene, and finds that he is drifting in a gondola. As the rhythmical strokes of the gondolier direct him and the poet down the Grand Canal of Venice — "how light we go, how soft we skim" — he sees the Ca' d'Oro shimmering in the bright, morning sun. They float slowly onward, past the Rialto Bridge, and onward, around the wide bend in the Canal that leads to the Bacino — "past we glide, and past, and past." Poliphilo has never seen Venice as he sees it on this morning — "a clear city on a sea-site in a light that shines from behind the sun." All her buildings stand in pristine freshness — "their very mass is a kind of illumination. They are illustrious with being." The sky is of the purest blue, and the air seems to have a texture, like that of soft velvet. The waters of the Grand Canal are liquid gold, and the colors of the sky and of the roseate marbles of the palaces dance upon its surface. Santa Maria della Salute appears on his right-hand side — "She glows, she sings in silvery radiance." Colored reflections of the golden water play harmoniously upon its marble surfaces as if to some unheard music. Passing the Dogana, all white in the sun, he sees San Giorgio Maggiore in the distance, "with a shimmering of pearl and silver, triumphant upon the waters." The nobility of its facade stands grandly magnified in the light, a nobility of stone amplified by a largesse of light.

The poet gestures to the gondolier, and he, in obedience to her silent command, turns the craft towards the Molo. As the Palazzo Ducale and the palaces along the Riva degli Schiavone come into view, Poliphilo's heart beats wildly, for Venice appears "like fabrics of enchantment piled to Heaven." The gondolier pulls the bark alongside the Molo and holds it steady as the pilgrim and the poet disembark. Poliphilo turns to take the poet's hand, and as she steps gracefully from the gondola, he notices how lightly she treads the stones, so lightly, in fact, that she appears to float.

The poet leads him into the Piazzetta towards the twin columns of Saint Theodore and the winged lion. Gazing between those ever-vigilant sentinels, he sees the arch below the Torre dell'Orologio, and the spring of its curve, as he contemplates it, somehow catches and expresses the elegance and strength of its columns, and these tall vertical masses, in turn, enhance the space of the arch, lending it a presence it otherwise would lack. Each part of the wondrous structure echoes the *virtù* of the buildings around it, and all in concert express a splendid *concinnitas*.

As the poet draws nearer the space between the columns in the Piazzetta, there appears, faintly at first, but with increasing clarity, a dark hole, like the mouth of a cave. As she is about to lead Poliphilo through this opening and into the darkness, he slows his pace, and the poet, feeling his resistance says, "Fear not! No harm will come to you here." With these words his courage returns, and he and the poet step over the threshold and into the cavernous obscurity, where a cold rain steadily falls.

Poliphilo sees there a crowd of people wandering about aimlessly, seemingly oblivious to the rain and perpetual night, each self-absorbed, as if trying to remember something of great importance. The women in this milling crowd are dressed in furs and rare fabrics, and the men also wear costly clothing. All have jewelled rings weighing down their fingers, and all wear necklaces, bracelets, anklets and ornaments for the hair. Some carry huge sacks of money, jewels and gold. Presently, a ravishingly beautiful woman catches sight of the poet and draws closer to her. At a distance, she appears as substantial and as solid as any other being, but the closer she moves towards Poliphilo's companion, the more ghostly she seems to grow, until, at last, standing before the poet, she appears a mere shadow. Pointing to Poliphilo, the indignant shade speaks: "Surely he is not one of us! He has no wealth." The poet, in a voice filled

with pity, replies: "His wealth is not your wealth, nor yours his."
With that the shadow rudely turns and rejoins her fellow shades.
Poliphilo asks the poet, "Who are they?" and she explains, "They
have forgotten those who grow the grain, those who mill it and
those who transport it to the City. They are blind to the pattern, be-
lieving the illusion that they are separate from the City and not
responsible to it." Then she takes his hand again. Together they
step forward, and as they do so, the shadow and her people, the
darkness, and the rain disappear, and he once again beholds the
morning light.

Near the center of the Piazzetta, the poet pauses abruptly and
turns toward the Ducal Palace. The pink and white incrustation of
the wall supported on two rows of columns, one above the other, is
no mere geometric pattern; rather it reveals a harmony that underlies all of Venice (or so it seems to Poliphilo), as if the unrelenting
Venetian pulse were suddenly arrested and made visible.
Surmounting this colored harmony and gazing out toward the sea,
the carved figure of Justice stands between two obelisks, her
polished bronze sword flashing in the sunlight. Turning to the
poet, Poliphilo beholds her enthralled by the figure, which now
looks at her, and the poet's face is transfigured in that moment of
mutual regard by a radiance greater than that which he had seen
there before. The unexpected likeness between them, poet and
Justice, is such that they seem twin sisters, each admiring the
perfection of her own beauty in that of the other.

After a short while, Poliphilo asks his friend again about the
shadows imprisoned in the dark place between the columns, for he
cannot forget them. She turns slowly around to view the Biblioteca
and Jacopo Sansovino's facade and speaks: "The wealth of Jacopo's
facade reveals the wealth of knowledge bound and shelved within.
Rightly, we honor the Florentine, and courteously, we also honor
that imagination that correctly sets stone upon stone, and that
imagination that carefully tends the animals in whose hide the
books are bound. The roots of the city extend far and wide, and the
city is its people, who are the city and who serve it. These buildings
express the city."

The Poet again takes Poliphilo's hand and leads him towards
the church of San Marco. As they walk past the Porta della Carta
and the Campanile, the Piazza begins to come into view, and he
hears what can only be described as a song without words. Standing
with his back to the central portal of the church and taking in the

vast expanse before him, he understands that the music is of the three facades surrounding the square. The visible harmony of the architecture is miraculously transformed into music. So great is his delight at this marvel of stone-song, or musical stone, that for a few moments he, transported, forgets all else.

Presently, however, he once again feels the gentle touch of the poet's hand upon his arm and looks towards her, noticing, as he does so, an old man standing with them and facing the central entrance to the church. This man, with his sad face and snow-white beard, his wide brimmed hat and camel-hair overcoat, speaks in a dry, cracking voice: "Greed is the worm in the heart of the city," and again, after a pause, as if to explain further, "There is no greed in true art." As the old man speaks, a deep silence and thick mist engulfs the three of them, and the poet, sensing Poliphilo's astonishment, explains, "He loved the city well but saw not clearly. The city imposes no man's system upon itself. The city lives and grows in the heart and reason of those who serve it, and not the least servant is denied his place here." Then, the old man, seemingly in answer to the Poet, says, "Beyond the order of the city resides LOVE," and she replies, "Civic order is not the city, although the city is well ordered. AMOR is CARITAS or it is little," and, turning to Poliphilo, adds, "When understanding comes to him, he will enter in." With those words she points to the doorway of the church and taking him by the hand, leads Poliphilo through it. As she does so, the mist of the old man's words evaporates, and the morning light shines brightly again, but not as brilliantly as the light within the narthex of the church, where the two now stand.

The poet with an expression full of kindness tells Poliphilo, "Here I must leave you in other hands. Your obedience to her is your only hope. Farewell." She then moves through the portal again, past the old man, still staring blankly into the church, and into the Piazza, leaving the pilgrim with a feeling of sadness and loneliness. Soon, however, he is startled back to his senses, for at the top of the steep stairs leading from the narthex to the church proper, he sees a woman, who, for some unfathomable reason makes him think of water — "marvelously spring-livened; spring of the world, spring of the heart; joy of spring water, joy." Words will not describe her beauty, nor how the beauty of her face and body express the beauty of her soul. She is gentle and delicate, yet strong and mighty in her strength. So great is his reverence for her that Poliphilo falls to his knees in adoration. She bids him to stand up, "Come, pilgrim, rise, for now you only dream, and I shall teach you what I may." He stands upright immediately and, ascending the stairs, fixes his gaze upon her.

She wears a light blue tunic, which partly reveals and partly hides her divinely proportioned form, and a mantle as green as new grass. Both tunic and mantle are shot through with tiny flecks of gold. The light behind her long blonde hair creates a kind of halo, and she seems truly angelic, but she seems, too, more real, more substantial than anyone he has ever encountered. As Poliphilo cautiously draws closer to her at the top of the stairs, she moves aside slightly, allowing him an unobstructed view of the interior of the church. The light there is so bright that he must close his eyes, then squint to see. As he grows accustomed to this brightness, he opens his eyes wider and sees a shaft of light streaming through the window in the transept and filling the altar-end of the church, a light that is mysteriously duller than the interior light. All around the golden walls sparkle, as gold-foil sparkles in the sun, only more intensely. The air here is far purer and sweeter than any he has ever breathed while awake and is filled with a faint, though almost intoxicating, fragrance. Above, an unseen choir chants a song of unrestrained praise.

The lady takes Poliphilo's hand, and as she does so, his heart, mind, and soul are filled with her serenity, as if she has purified their murky contents. She leads him forward down the nave, pausing about midway to instruct him, "See the bits of marble in the floor, how they make a pattern, here organic and there geometric, and see how they dance. See the tesserae in the golden walls, how each represents a moment in time, here preserved. See how the smaller moments seen together form the greater, and how the greater are there in the smaller." Still holding his hand, for which courtesy he is most grateful (for he is fearfully cautious), she leads him further down the nave towards the altar.

As they approach the iconostasis, they again pause, and she directs him to contemplate the carved figures lining the top of the screen. In the center is the Cross, and on each side of it are seven figures. As Poliphilo looks along the row, the figures appear to come to life and a quiet grief seems to emanate from them as they lament the death of the Logos. Looking with ever increasing intensity, Poliphilo is overwhelmed by the hands of Saint Mary and how they express the torment of her being, and by the hands of Saint John, one of which he presses to his head, as if to dispel an agony of reason. Lastly, the pilgrim gazes upon the Paraclete, but the image, so skillfully wrought, remains but a figure carved in stone.

Disappointed he turns hopefully to his companion, who now stands directly below the Cross on the top step of the stairs leading to the opening in the iconostasis. She beckons him, and ascending the steps, he stands facing her. She looks deeply into his eyes and says, "Fear not! Now you dream, and I will teach you what I may." Then, with an ever so gentle smile, she says, "Look into my eyes and tell me what you see." Heartened, Poliphilo looks into her radiant eyes and sees the tree — now bare, yet forever blossoming; green and eternally autumnal. The lady instructs him to look once more.

> "All love is one eternal Love,
> all pain, one everlasting Pain,
> but Time and Pain are consumed
> in Love's eternal flame."

And he awoke.

6: Poetic License

NEAR THE MIDDLE of the seventeenth century, Paolo Veronese's enormous painting for the refectory of the friars of Santi Giovanni e Paolo in Venice, the so-called *Feast in the House of Levi* (plate 21), and the circumstances in which it was created were described by the Venetian art historian and critic, Carlo Ridolfi (1594–1658).Veronese, Ridolfi says, painted the picture to replace a *Last Supper* by Titian that had been destroyed by fire. He also refers to the person who commissioned the painting.

> Fra Andrea de' Buoni, desiring to replace the picture [i.e., Titian's] offered Paolo a certain amount of money that came from alms and penitence offerings; a sum that no gentleman of today would accept even to prime such a large canvas. Being unable to spend more money, the poor friar finally moved Paolo by his prayers to agree, more from a desire of glory than of gain, to so large a task. The scene is represented beneath a spacious loggia, divided into three arches, outside of which beautiful structures of palaces that delight the eye are seen. In the center sits the Savior, facing Him is Levi, dressed in purple, and with them many Publicans are sitting and others mixed in with the Apostles, and these comprise very rare heads to singular effect and various portraits, among them the above-mentioned Fra Andrea in a corner, with a table-napkin over his shoulder. For this one likeness one could get the cost of the entire work. Among the things to admire is the figure of the host, leaning on a pedestal, in which other than singularly indicating the quality of his personage, is the fresh flesh that seems alive. Next to him is an Ethiopian servant, in Moroccan costume and basket in hand, expressing a laughter that moves to laughter anyone who sees him. The whole work, in short, is managed with as much surpassing skill as is possible in this genre, for Paolo did not want to have it on his conscience, nor give material

to the Frate for regret at having ill-spent his money.[1]

Ridolfi effectively evokes the *grandezza* and air of luxury in Veronese's painting. Indeed, the painting is so overwhelmingly vital that we still marvel that the artist was summoned on July 18, 1573, shortly after he had finished the picture, before the Tribunal of the Inquisition in regard to it. [2]

The document recording his appearance before the Inquisition consists of some notes hastily taken by a scribe present at the hearing, and even though they are sometimes imprecise and apparently do not record all that was said, they give a fairly good idea of both the accusations brought against the painter and his defense.[3] The notes have been known to scholars for well over a century, but no one has recognized the importance of what the artist has to say in them about Michelangelo's *Last Judgment* on the altar-wall of the Sistine Chapel (plate 26). This is surprising, for Veronese's reference to Michelangelo's painting lies at the very heart of his defense,

---

[1] Carlo Ridolfi, *Le maraviglie dell'arte*, ed. Detlev von Hadeln. 2 vols. (Rome, 1965), 1:313–4: "...Frà Andrea de' Buoni, desideroso di veder rinovata la Pittura, offerì à Paolo per questo effetto certa quantità di danaro, che avvanzato di elemosine e di confessioni haveva, prezzo che per avventura non si accettarebbe da un galant'huomo ne' presenti tempi per lo imprimere una così grand tela. Ma non potendo il povero Frate spender di più, sforzato Paolo da preghi, lo volle in fine compiacere così gran carica, spinto più dal desio della gloria, che dell'utile. L'apparecchio è finto sotto à spatiosa Loggia, in tre grand'archi compartita, fuor de' quali si mirano belle strutture de' Palagi, che rendono dilettevole veduta. Nel mezzo posa il Salvatore, al dirimpetto Levi vestitto di purpurea veste, e seco siedono molti Publicani, & altri mescolati con gli Apostoli, ne' quali compose rarissime teste in singolari effetti, e vari ritrasse Frate Andrea sudetto in un canto con la salvietta sopra la spalla, della cui effigie si trarebbe di vantaggio ciò, che fù speso nell'opera; e trà le cose d'ammiratione è la figura dell'Hoste appoggiato ad un piedestallo, che oltre il divisar singolarmente le qualità del personaggio, è di così fresche carni, che par vivo, e gli è vicino un servo Etiope con habito moresco e cesta in mano, che mostra di ridere, che muove à riso, chi lo mira. L'opera tutta in fine è maneggiata con grande maestria, quanto in questo genere si può fare, non volendo Paolo rimettervi di conscienza, ne dar materia à Frate di dolersi, di haver mal impiegato il suo danaro. (My translation.)

[2] See Sandra Moschini Marconi, *Gallerie dell'Accademia di Venezia: Opere d'arte del secolo XVI* (Rome, 1962), 83–5, and Teresio Pignatti, *Veronese*, 2 vols. (Venice, 1976), 1:136 cat. no. 177. See also, André Chastel, *Art of the Italian Renaissance*, trans. Peter and Linda Murray (New York, 1988), 208–27.

[3] See Appendix A.

which rests largely on the Horation notion of "poetic license."[4]

The proceedings against the artist begin with a question about his name and surname, which he gives as Paolo Caliari of Verona. Questioned about his profession, he responds that he "paint[s] and makes figures."[5] Asked why he has been called before the Tribunal, Veronese says that he does not know, but that he can well imagine. The prior of the church of Santi Giovanni e Paolo, he explains, was ordered by the Tribunal to have a dog (still visible in the lower center of the painting) replaced with a figure of the Magdalene. The painter, who did not feel that such a figure would serve just as well as the dog, had refused to make the change.

We cannot be certain of the reason why the Tribunal wanted a Magdalene in place of the dog or why Veronese would not make the change, but his response to the next question put to him suggests a possible answer. When asked to give the subject matter of his painting, he identifies it as the Last Supper. Now the Magdalene was not present at the Last Supper but was present at the feast in the house of Simon the Leper and at the feast in the house of the Pharisee. Thus, for the artist to have included a figure of her would have rather arbitrarily changed the subject matter of his painting.

When Veronese answers the question about what his painting represents, he says that it depicts "the Last Supper, which Jesus Christ took with his apostles in the house of Simon."[6] Because the

---

[4] The only scholar to make more than a passing comment on Veronese's remarks about Michelangelo's painting is Gino Fogolari, "Il processo dell'Inquisizione a Paolo Veronese," *Archivio veneto* 17 (1935): 378–9, who, however, misinterprets their significance.

[5] For the significance of Veronese's reply in relation to the Arte dei Depentori, see David Rosand, *Painting in Cinquecento Venice: Titian, Veronese, Tintoretto* (New Haven and London, 1982), 10–11.

[6] For recent discussions of the painting as a representation of the Last Supper, see Fehl, "Veronese and the Inquisition: A Study of the Subject-Matter of the so-called 'Feast in the House of Levi'," *Gazette des Beaux-Arts*, 6th ser. 58 (1961):325–48; Creighton Gilbert, "Last Suppers and Their Refectories," in *The Pursuit of Holiness in Late Medieval and Renaissance Religion*, ed. Charles Trinkhaus and H. A. Oberman (Leiden, 1974), 397–400; Rosand, *Painting in Cinquecento Venice*, 163–7; and Brian T. D'Argaville, "Inquisition and Metamorphosis: Paolo Veronese and the 'Ultima Cena' of 1573," *RACAR* 16 (1989):43–8. See also Philipp Fehl and Marilyn Perry, "Painting and the Inquisition at Venice: Three Forgotten Files," in *Interpretazioni veneziane: Studi di storia dell'arte in onore di Michelangelo Muraro*, ed. David Rosand (Venice, 1984), 371–83.

precise location of the Last Supper is not known, and because the artist locates the event in the house of Simon, some feel that he purposely wanted to appear ignorant of Biblical matters so as to make his inquisitors believe that he was a naive painter and not responsible for his actions.[7] This is not very likely because it is inconsistent with the rest of Veronese's defense, which is perfectly reasonable. Indeed, the record "shows Paolo's gentle irony, composure, and intellectual superiority to his judges in every answer."[8] We should remark, too, that the artist does not further identify the particular Simon to whom he refers, except to say, later on, that he was wealthy. Still, it is clear that he represented the Last Supper.[9]

Veronese is next asked a series of questions about the physical particulars of his work. It is, he says, a painting on canvas located in the refectory of Santi Giovanni e Paolo and measures about seventeen feet in height by thirty-nine feet in width. Now the artist is asked to explain his representation of certain "ministri" or servants. He first names Simon (perhaps the figure seated on this side of the table under the central arch), who is the master of the inn where the scene takes place, then a steward (perhaps the figure with his arms outstretched, standing just to the left of the central arch), whom he "imagined had come for his entertainment to see how things were going at the table" ("il quale ho finto ch[e]l sia venuto p[er] suo diporto a veder come vanno le cose della t[av]ola"), and ends by saying that he does not recall all of the figures.

---

[7] See, for example, Percy H. Osmund, *Paolo Veronese: His Career and Work* (London, 1927), 69, who writes that "Paolo certainly need not have been ignorant of the Gospel narrative; he was probably feigning ignorance which would disarm suspicion"; Anthony Blunt, *Artistic Theory in Italy, 1450-1600* (Oxford, 1940), 116, who says that Veronese "argues ingeniously"; Elizabeth G. Holt, ed., *A Documentary History of Art*, 2 vols. (Princeton, 1982), 2: 67 note 2, who writes that "Paolo seems to [feign] ignorance and to have little interest in the doctrinal significance of his pictures"; and Paul H. D. Kaplan, "Veronese's Last 'Supper'," *Arte veneta* 41 (1987):51, who says that Veronese's replies "were sometimes almost flippant."

[8] W. R. Rearick, *The Art of Paolo Veronese, 1528-1588* (Washington, D. C. and London, 1988), 104.

[9] Cecil Gould, "Veronese's Greatest Feast: The Inter-action of Iconographic and Aesthetic Factors," *Arte Veneta* 43 (1989–90): 85–88, argues that the artist originally intended the painting to represent a Last Supper, then changed the subject matter to a supper in the house of Simon before he was called to the Tribunal.

When next asked about other "suppers" he had painted, Veronese first names, without giving specific titles, his *Feast in the House
of the Pharisee* (plate 22) for the refectory of Santi Nazzaro e Celso
at Verona (now in the Pinacoteca, Turin), and then his *Wedding
Feast at Cana* (plate 23) for the refectory of San Giorgio Maggiore in
Venice (now in the Louvre, Paris). At this point he is interrupted
by his interrogator, who points out that he was asked about the
"Supper of the Lord," implying that the last-mentioned painting
does not fall into that category, perhaps because it does not represent a supper for Christ, but a meal that he attended as a guest.
Continuing, Veronese further names, again without specific titles,
his *Feast in the House of Simon the Leper* (plate 24) for the refectory of the Servi in Venice (now in the Louvre, Paris); another *Feast
in the House of the Pharisee* (plate 25) for the refectory of San
Sebastiano also in Venice (now in the Brera, Milan); and finally a
lost painting for the fathers of the Magdalene in Padua. We should
note that three of the identifiable paintings named by Veronese
contain a figure of the Magdalene. This fact strongly suggests that
the artist knew very well the difference between the Last Supper
and the other suppers of Christ recorded in the New Testament.

Perhaps hoping to confuse the artist, the interrogator again
changes the kind of question he asks. He inquires about the significance of a figure with a bleeding nose (on the stairway to the left
holding a cloth in his hand), and Veronese responds that he painted a servant who has met with some accident. The artist is then
queried about the significance of certain soldiers dressed as Germans (on the stairway opposite the man with the nosebleed), to
which question he replies, "We painters take the same license that
poets and jesters take" ("Nui pittori si pigliamo licentia, che si
pigliano i poeti e i matti") and continues that he depicted the German soldiers because they serve an appropriate purpose. He had
been told, he says, that the master of the house in which the scene
takes place was grand and rich and would, therefore, it seemed to
him, have such attendants.

Gino Fogolari once suggested that in claiming the same license
that poets take, Veronese is recalling a certain line in Horace's *Ars
poetica* that claims equal power of inventive imagination or poetic
license for poets and painters — *pictoribus atque poetis quidlibet
audendi semper fuit aequas potestas* — a power that Horace
thought should be used with restraint and in conformity with

nature.[10] Fogolari was correct, but the idea expressed by Horace had gained a rich and complex significance by the time of Veronese, a significance that helps us to understand better the artist's defense.

Medieval writers on art upheld Horace's view of license and propriety in the creation of fantastic images, but Renaissance art theorists, beginning with Cennino Cennini, tended to emphasize either the idea of license or that of propriety and restraint. Cennini explains in his *Il libro dell'arte* that painting combines *fantasia* and manual operations in order "to discover things not seen, things hiding under the shadow of nature," and the painter must show forth in his art "that which does not exist as if it does exist."[11] Painting, Cennini continues, deserves to be ranked just below pure science and to be crowned with poetry, because just as the poet has the right and liberty to compose and bind together "as he pleases, according to his will," so, too, does the painter have the freedom to make "a standing figure or a seated one, or one that is half man and half horse," as he pleases, according to his *fantasia*. Cennini is speaking here of two kinds of artistic liberty. Unlike Horace, who lamented the creation of such chimerical figures as mermaids, Cennini affirms the license of poets and painters to create that kind of fantastic image, specifically a centaur. He is also affirming the freedom of painters, as well as of poets, to compose their works as they wish, according to their will. The painter, for example, may depict "standing figures or seated ones," as he wishes.

Although many writers on art understood Horace's advice as above all a call to restraint and propriety in the creation of images, the right to freedom of invention was claimed by artists other than Cennini, who, we should recall, was himself a painter. A follower of the fifteenth-century Florentine artist, Benozzo Gozzoli, for instance, inscribed a version of Horace's dictum on one of his notebooks — *Pictoribus atque poetis semper fuit et erit aequa potestas* ("Painters and poets have always had and will always have the same power"); that is to say, poets and painters have equal right to freedom of invention.[12] Leonardo da Vinci, who in his notes on the sister arts reverses the formula, writes that "poets like painters

---

10 Fogolari, "Il processo dell'Inquisizione," 371.

11 Cennini, *Il libro dell'arte*, 3–4.

12 For this notebook, see Arthur E. Popham, "A Book of Drawings of the School of Benozzo Gozzoli," *Old Master Drawings* 4 (1929–1930): 53–4.

are free in their inventions" ("se 'l poeta è libero come 'l pittore nelle inventioni, le sue finitione non sonno di tanta satisfatione alli homini, quanto le pitture"), and Michelangelo, too, as David Summers has recently shown, insisted upon the artist's right to dare.13

In Venice, the right to freedom of invention was no less important for artists. For example, when Isabella d'Este attempted to impose a *storia* that had been already composed upon Giovanni Bellini, he refused to paint it.14 Later, she sought the aid of the poet Pietro Bembo, at the time living in Venice, who was to try again to persuade Bellini to paint a *poesia* for the walls of her famous *studiolo* in Mantua. Bembo replied that the invention must be accommodated to the artist's *fantasia*, for he does not like many written instructions and is accustomed, "always to wander at will in his paintings," so that they will satisfy both himself and the viewer:

> The invention, which you write I should discover for the design, will need to be accommodated to the imagination of him who makes it, because he wants that many instructions do not do damage to his style; he is accustomed, he says, always to wander at his will in his paintings, so that they will satisfy himself as well as those who view them.15

A similar attitude toward invention was a short while later expressed by the sixteenth century Venetian painter and art theorist Paolo Pino. Pino divides the art of painting into its conventional parts, *invenzione, disegno*, and *colorire*, except that significantly, he discusses *disegno* before invention. Certainly there is nothing unusual about Pino's understanding of drawing and coloring. His

---

13 *The Literary Works of Leonardo da Vinci*, ed. Jean Paul Richter, 3rd ed., 2 vols. (New York, 1970), 1:57; and Summers, *Michelangelo*, 103–43.

14 For the documents related to this phase of Isabella's dealings with Bellini, see Clifford M. Brown and Anna Maria Lorenzoni, *Isabella d'Este and Lorenzo da Pavia: Documents for the History of Art and Culture in Renaissance Mantua* (Geneva, 1982), 59–167.

15 Pietro Bembo, *Lettere I (1492-1507)*, ed. Ernesto Travi (Bologna, 1987), 196, no. 209: "La inventione che mi scrive...che io truovi al disegno, bisognerà che s'accomodi alla fantasia di lui che l'ha a fare, il quale ha piacere che molto signati termini non si diano al suo stile, uso, come dice, di sempre vagare a sua voglia nelle pitture, che quanto è in lui, possano soddisfare a chi le mira."

definition of invention, however, is quite remarkable, for it emphasizes the autonomy of the artist. Painting, he says, is "really poetry, that is, invention." Indeed, the painter should discover ("truovare"— the same word used by Bembo) "poesie" or "historie" on his own.[16]

Vasari isolates the element of *fantasia* in Venetian art, especially in certain works of Giorgione and Tintoretto. Giorgione, he says, was commissioned to paint frescoes on the Fondaco dei Tedeschi as he pleased ("secondo la sua fantasia") and that there the artist depicted "figures according to his *fantasia*" ("farvi figure a sua fantasia"), with the result that no one, including Vasari, was able to understand their meaning.[17] Likewise, in his comments on the works of Tintoretto, added to the *Vita* of Battista Franco, he refers a number of times to the artist's *fantasia*. The manner of Tintoretto's paintings is "quick, resolute, capricious and extravagant," and his scenes are "fantastic compositions." Indeed, he goes beyond extravagance in his "new and fanciful inventions." A specific instance of Tintoretto's fantasy is his *Last Judgment* for the church of Santa Maria dell'Orto, which contains, Vasari says, a "fantastic" ("capricciosa") and "extravagant" invention.[18]

Veronese, then, in responding to the Tribunal, is not simply recalling Horace. Rather he places himself in the deep tradition of "poetic license" claimed by artists as far back as Cennini and probably before. His claim to "poetic license" is Horatian, however, to the extent that he says that he exercises it within the bounds of propriety, as is suggested when he explains that the soldiers dressed as Germans are appropriate because they are attendants of the master of the house, who was great and rich.

If we are able to make some sense of Veronese's claim that artists have the same license as poets, his comparison of painters and fools ("matti"), or jesters, in terms of poetic license is rather more difficult to explain.[19] A possible clue to his meaning, however, may

---

[16] Paolo Pino, *Dialogo della Pittura* (Venice, 1548). I have used the text of Pino's treatise in *Trattati*, 1:115–6.

[17] Vasari-Milanesi, 4:91.

[18] Ibid., 6:588–94.

[19] For a discussion of the association of jesters and poets, see Enid Welsford, *The Fool: His Social and Literary History* (Gloucester [Mass.], 1966), 76–112.

be found in the *Novelle* of the poet and humanist, Matteo Bandello (ca. 1480–1561). There Isabella da Casate describes at some length the famous Gonnella, court-jester to the Marchese Niccolò d'Este of Ferrara, and his foolish methods. Isabella says that the

jokes and buffooneries that he carried out were not the products of insanity or small intelligence, but were born of the vivacity, acuteness and sublimity of his talent so that he did everything thoughtfully; and as he was planning to make some joke, he considered the nature of those whom he wished to fool and the pleasure the Marchese would consequently derive from it. And of the many he carried out at various times, I have never heard that he played one on the Marchese. This Gonnella was of a very pensive nature, and when he found himself alone, he always dreamed up and imagined some jest, and first planned them out to himself three or four times before putting his hands to the pasta.[20]

Isabella suggests that Gonnella exercised a certain decorum — a fool's decorum, we might say — when planning his tricks, and this sense of appropriateness is comparable to that of Veronese. Just as the artist considered how the elements of his painting related to his subject matter, Gonnella was careful about the relation between his jest and the character of the person upon whom it would be played. Perhaps it was this sense of decorum that prevented him from making fun of Niccolò d'Este or perhaps it was only common sense. In any case, he exercised his imagination within the limits imposed upon him by his subject, just as Veronese did.

The inquisitor, who no doubt would have been aware of the kind of pranks jesters like Gonnella played, now questions Veronese about the buffoon with a parrot on his arm (just to the left of

---

[20] Matteo Bandello, *Tutte le opere*, ed. Francesco Flora, 2 vols. (Verona, 1943), 2:774: "...le buffonerie e piacevolezze che faceva non procedevano nè da pazzia nè da poco cervello, ma nascevano de la vivacità, acutezza e sublimità de l'ingegno che in lui era, perciò che il tutto faceva pensatamente; e come si deliberava fare alcuna galanteria, considerava la natura di quelli che beffar voleva e il piacer che ne poteva consequire il signor marchese. E di molte che a diversi tempi fece, io ve ne vuo' dire una che a esso marchese da lui fu fatta. Era di natura sua molto pensoso esso Gonnella; per questo, come si trovava solo, sempre chimerizzava e si imaginava alcuna piacevolezza, e tra sè prima la ordiva tre o quattro volte avanti che le mai mettesse in pasta [IV, 23]."

center at the head of the stairs) in his painting and to what effect he had painted it. "For ornament, as one does" ("per orname[n]to, come si fa"), is the artist's reply. By "ornament" he means not so much beauty as such, but embellishment.[21] The buffoon, Veronese says, was put in the painting in order to embellish the scene. His examiner goes on to inquire about the apostles and their significance and asks him what Saint Peter, who is seated next to Christ on His right-hand side, and Saint John are doing. Saint Peter, the artist explains, is quartering the lamb, and Saint John is holding a plate to receive a portion of the meat. Another figure (visible between the columns just to the left of Saint Peter), he says, is picking his teeth. Veronese is then asked whom he truly believes one would have found at the Last Supper, and responds that he believes one would have found Christ and his apostles. But, he says, "if some space presents itself in a painting, I adorn it with figures according to the invention" ("se nel quadro li avanza spacio, io l'adorno di figure [se]condo le invenzioni"). Veronese here means that if there is extra space in a painting, he will adorn or embellish it with figures that are in some way related to the invention or subject matter.

His examiner follows up by asking if the artist was commissioned to paint buffoons, Germans, and similar things. Veronese responds that he was not; he was commissioned to make the painting, which is large and capable of holding many figures, according to his own lights, as he pleased. In response, the inquisitor wonders if it is usual for painters to make their ornaments in conformity with the significance of the subject matter and principal figures, or do they make the ornaments according to their "fantasia" or imagination, without discretion or judgement ("Se li ornam[en]ti che lui pittore è solito di fare dintorno le pitture o quadri...le solito di fare convenienti et proportionati all materia et figure principali o veram[en]te a caso beneplacito secondo ch[e] li viene in fantasia senza alcuna discrittione et giudito"). This question, which in essence asks Veronese if he holds to Horace's dictum, was intended, perhaps, to test the painter's sincerity and consistency, for he has already claimed the right to freedom of invention within the bounds of propriety. Indeed, it must have come as no surprise when Veronese answered that he makes his pictures according to what is appropriate as far as his intellect is able.

---

21 For Veronese's use of the word "ornamento," see Summers, *Michelangelo,* 496 note 104.

When he is asked if it appears appropriate that at the Last Supper of the Lord he paints buffoons, drunkards, Germans, dwarfs and other scurrilous things, the artist responds that it is not. "Why, then, have you painted them?" he is asked. "I made them because I determined before hand that they are outside the place where the supper is taking place" ("l'ho fatto p[er]che presuppono ch[e] questi sieno fuori d[el] luoco dovesi fa la cena"). Part of Veronese's defense, then, is that drunken Germans, buffoons, and dwarfs are not appropriate at the Last Supper, but that in his painting there is a separation between the area in which the holy meal takes place and the area in which the offensive figures appear.[22]

At this point the artist's examiner reveals the crux of the matter. "Do you not know," he demands, "that in Germany and other places infested with heresy they are beginning with diverse paintings full of scurrilities and inventions similar to yours to mock and vituperate and make ridiculous the things of the Holy Catholic Church in order to teach false doctrine to stupid and ignorant people?" Veronese, it seems, was called before the Tribunal because someone thought that there might be hidden significance of a Protestant nature in the allegedly scurrilous figures of his painting, specifically the buffoon and the German soldiers, which might be seen to mock the holy subject matter. That person's concern, if in fact it was only one person who complained, we should note, is in line with the Church's official position insofar as it echoes portions of the decree (*De invocatione, veneratione et reliquiis sanctorum, et sacris imaginibus*) of the twenty-fifth session of the Council of Trent, held in December of 1563, which allows "no representation of false doctrines and such as might be the occasion of grave error to the uneducated [to] be exhibited," and specifies that in works of art there may not appear anything that is "disorderly or unbecoming and confusedly arranged, nothing that is profane, nothing disrespectful, since holiness becometh the house of God."[23]

Veronese, who agrees that the teaching of false doctrine is wrong, then appears to change the nature of his defense. He says that he is "obliged to follow what his superiors have done," and

---

22 For the importance of Veronese's distinction between the area in which the Supper takes place and the surrounding but separate space, see Rosand, *Painting in Cinquecento Venice*, 163–7.

23 Henry Joseph Schroeder, trans., *Canons and Decrees of the Council of Trent* (Saint Louis and London, 1941), 216–7, 484–5.

when asked what he is referring to, he points to the example of Michelangelo's *Last Judgment* (plate 26) in the Sistine Chapel. "Michelangelo in Rome," he says, "inside the pontifical chapel has painted our Lord Jesus Christ, his mother and Saint John, Saint Peter and the celestial court, all of which are shown in the nude, from the Virgin Mary on, in various acts with little reverence."

The artist here echoes the attack on Michelangelo's painting made by Pietro Aretino, who lived in Venice, that the postures and genitalia of the figures in the *Last Judgment* do not show reverence for the holy place in which they are depicted and are better suited to a brothel. Aretino claims that Michelangelo, a Christian, is worse in this regard than the pagans, who in their statues clothed Diana and had Venus cover "the parts that one should not see" with her hands. The artist, Aretino says, "values art more than the faith" and "holds for a royal spectacle not only the lack of decorum in the martyrs and virgins but the gesture of carrying [men] off by their genitals, so that even [those in] the brothel would close their eyes so as not to see it."[24]

Veronese cites Michelangelo's fresco as an example for his own work, but the examiner will hear of it. He tells the artist, in the form of a question, that in a painting of the Last Judgment "one does not presume clothing and similar things"; therefore "it is not necessary to paint clothing." Furthermore, there is nothing in Michelangelo's figures "that is not of the spirit; there are no buffoons, no dogs, no weapons, nor similar buffoonery." The point is that Michelangelo's work is spiritual, that his nudes are not indecorous in relation to their subject matter. Therefore, his painting could not properly have served as an example for Veronese's picture.

We should remark here that the inquisitor does not address the issue of whether or not Michelangelo's nudes are indecorous in relation to their setting.

The inquisitor understands Veronese to suggest that Michelangelo is like one of those artists who compose their pictures according to their *fantasia* without discretion or judgment, but that is not what the artist is really saying. What he means, instead, is that his painting is similar to the *Last Judgment* to the extent that both are indecorous in relation to the location in which they are painted, the refectory of Santi Giovanni e Paolo and the Sistine Chapel, respectively. Veronese, in other words, is willing to concede that

24 Gaye and Reumont, *Carteggio inedito*, 332–5.

his buffoon, dwarf, and soldiers, like Michelangelo's nudes, are inappropriate to the place where they are found, but pleads innocent to the perhaps more serious charge that they are indecorous in relation to the subject matter of the painting because they are removed from the place where the Supper takes place.

His inquisitor seemingly misses Veronese's point and while ignoring the charge made by Aretino and others that Michelangelo's nudes are inappropriate for their setting, defends them in relation to their subject matter. In so doing, however, he unwittingly supports the artist's view that his buffoon and dwarf are appropriate to his subject matter because they appear outside the area where the Last Supper takes place. The inquisitor, then, implicitly confirms, surely without meaning to, that Michelangelo's painting is, just as Veronese contended, an appropriate parallel for his painting.

The interrogator at this point goes on to ask the artist if, because of Michelangelo's example or some other painting, he feels that he has done well in his own work. The record of the interrogation ends with Veronese's reply. He does not wish to defend his painting, but he thought that he was doing well in it. He did not consider all the things that have been pointed out to him, and he was certainly not thinking of confusing anyone, because, and here he repeats what he has said all along, "those figures of buffoons are outside the place where our Lord is" ("quelle figure di Buffoni sono di fuora d[e]l luogo dove è il n[ost]ro Sig[no]re").

Although Veronese was ultimately instructed to change certain portions of his composition, which are not specified in the document, within a three-month period and at his own expense, the painting as we see it today seems to be substantially as it was in 1573, except that an inscription (*Fecit D. Covi. Magnu. Levi Lucae Cap. V*) has been added, identifying the subject matter as the feast in the house of Levi.[25]

The record of Veronese's appearance before the Inquisition has been widely used as evidence in support of two contradictory views of his art. One view is that he was essentially a decorative artist more concerned with making a charming picture than with the significance of his subject matter. The other view is that he was very serious about his treatment of subject matter. As we have seen the

---

25 Cf. D'Argaville, "Inquisition and Metamorphoses," 45–8, who argues that Veronese did, indeed, substantially change the composition so that it would conform to the new subject matter.

record supports this latter view.[26] The Tribunal in essence accused
Veronese of depicting figures that were not appropriate to his
subject matter, and they suspected that these figures might have
some subversive significance. Veronese's principal defense is that
he, like other artists, has "poetic license," or freedom of invention,
and that he exercised this license with decorum in the representation of the offensive figures, which are appropriately related to the
subject matter, as he understood it, because they are outside the
area where the Last Supper takes place. As part of his defense he
names Michelangelo as an example to be followed. Like his own
painting, he suggests, the *Last Judgment* may lack decorum when
seen in relation to its surroundings, but, again like his own painting, as he implies and as his interrogator explains, the offensive
elements are appropriately related to the subject matter.

Veronese has been characterized as an artist who "thinks in
terms of beauty not of spiritual truth, and his object [it is said] was
to produce a magnificent pageant painting, not to illustrate a religious story."[27] This widely accepted opinion seems to arise from the
(by now) cliché that Venetian artists are primarily sensuous color-
ists, as distinguished from their Florentine counterparts, who excel
in the intellectual aspect of painting, *disegno*. That is to say, since
Veronese's paintings are beautifully and sensuously painted, then
he, the tacit argument runs, was merely sensuous and unintelli-
gent. As the record of his hearing before the Tribunal shows and as
his paintings demonstrate, this view is all together mistaken. Veronese presents his inquisitors with a reasonable and cogent defense,
a defense which reveals that, however sumptuous his art, however
intoxicating his colors, subject matter and its disposition, the very
meaning in his paintings, was of central concern for him, too.

---

[26] For the first view, see, for example, Blunt, *Artistic Theory*, 116; for the second, see Fehl, "Veronese and the Inquisition," 325–54; and Rosand,
Painting in Cinquecento Venice, 163–7. See also, Philipp Fehl, "Veronese's Decorum: Notes on the 'Marriage at Cana'," in *Art the Ape of Nature: Studies in
Honor of H. W. Janson*, eds. Moshe Barasch, Lucy Freeman Sandler, and Patricia Egan (New York, 1981), 341–65.

[27] Blunt, *Artistic Theory*, 116. Blunt's opinion is echoed by Hartt, *Italian Renaissance Art*, 627, who says that in the artist's Biblical scenes he was "concerned *only* with material food, and the material splendor of the setting and
the sumptuous costumes of the actors." (Author's emphasis.)

7: Critical Values — Cinquecento

FOR MORE THAN THREE centuries, until it was virtually destroyed on the night of 16 August 1867, Titian's *Martyrdom of Saint Peter Martyr* (1526–1530), then in the chapel of the Rosario in the church of Santi Giovanni e Paolo in Venice, was widely held to be not only one of the artist's best works, but one of the finest pictures of the Italian Renaissance.[1] Numerous copies of the altarpiece, including those by Annibale and Ludovico Carracci (now lost) and a print by Martino Rota (plate 27) attest to its popularity. So do the many written descriptions of it by some of the most prominent art historians and critics of the centuries preceding its destruction. Rota's print, especially, has helped latter-day art historians to recognize and to describe not only the importance of the painting for an understanding of Titian's development as an artist, but the influence of the work on subsequent art, such as Caravaggio's *Martyrdom of Saint Matthew* in the Contarelli Chapel in San Luigi dei Francesi in Rome.[2] The descriptions of Titian's painting, however, except where they provide data for the reconstruction of the circumstances surrounding the competition for the commission of the picture, have received relatively little attention. Perhaps this lack of attention is due to the fact that the descriptions are related to a

[1] For the circumstances surrounding the destruction of the painting and the reappearance of two, reputedly authentic fragments of it, see Eugenio Riccòmini, "Il capolavoro di Tiziano non era bruciato," *Giornale dell'arte* 7 (October 1989): 1–2. For the extant and lost copies of Titian's painting, see Harold E. Wethey, *The Paintings of Titian, I: The Religious Paintings* (London, 1969), 153–5, cat. no. 133. See also Francesco Sansovino, *Venetia: città nobilissima et singolare* (Venice, 1581), 23v, who relates that Titian's altarpiece replaced one by Jacobello del Fiore.

[2] For example, see, respectively, David Rosand, *Titian* (New York, 1978), 20–1 and Howard Hibbard, *Caravaggio* (New York), 1983, 106. See also Patricia Meilman, "Titian's Saint Peter Martyr and the Development of Altar Painting in Renaissance Venice," (Ph. D. Diss., Columbia University, 1989).

particular kind of writing known as ekphrasis.[3]

In its strictest sense the term ekphrasis refers to a rhetorical exercise defined by Hermogenes of Tarsus in the second century A. D. as the vivid, detailed account "of people, actions, times, places, seasons and many other things."[4] Among the "many other things" described by writers of ekphraseis are works of art, both real or imagined. For example, in the second and third centuries A. D., the two Philostratoi and Callistratus each wrote a book comprising a series of ekphrastic descriptions of works of art. In the Renaissance and after, ekphrastic descriptions were often part of a larger literary undertaking, such as a long poem (e.g., Dante's *Purgatorio*) or a prose narrative (e.g., Francesco Colonna's *Hypnerotomachia Poliphili*), but often appeared alone in the form of short poems on actual works of art (e.g., Jacopo Sadoleto's *De Laocoontis Statua*). Ekphrastic descriptions are also used as illustrative material in theoretical treatises on art, such as those by Leon Battista Alberti and Lodovico Dolce.[5] Students of art literature, then, broadly define ekphrasis as the verbal recreation or evocation of a work of art in prose or verse.

Although descriptive in nature and subject to literary conventions, ekphrasis should be considered a kind of art criticism. In practical criticism, which is not descriptive, the critic evaluates the merits and failures of a work of art according to specific criteria. For

[3] Paolo Pino, *Dialogo di pittura* [Venice, 1548], in *Trattati*, 137, says that Titian competed with Palma Vecchio for the commission; Carlo Ridolfi, *Le maraviglie dell'arte*, 2:167, adds Pordenone to the list of competitors; Francesco Scannelli, *Il microcosmo della pittura*, ed. Guido Guibbini (1657; reprint, Milan, 1966), 217, says that he saw three drawings connected to the commission in a private Bolognese collection, one each by Titian, Pordenone and Palma Vecchio. See also Marco Boschini, *La carta del navegar pittoresco*, ed. Anna Pallucchini (Venice, 1966), 222, who says that the friars of Santi Giovanni e Paolo were offered eighteen thousand *scudi* for the painting by Daniele Nis, but that the sale was forbidden by the Venetian senate under penalty of death. For a recent discussion of the documents concerning the painting, see André Chastel, *Art of the Italian Renaissance*, 170–87.

[4] See Michael Baxandall, *Giotto and the Orators: Humanist Observers of Painting in Italy and the Discovery of Pictorial Composition, 1350–1450* (Oxford, 1971), 85.

[5] For a discussion of ekphrasis in Alberti's treatise, see David Rosand, "Ekphrasis and the Renaissance of Painting: Observations on Alberti's Third Book," in *Florilegium Columbianum: Essays in Honor of Paul Oskar Kristeller*, ed. Karl-Ludwig Selig and Robert Somerville (New York, 1988), 147–63.

example, when Lorenzo da Pavia writes to Isabella d'Este about a *presepio* painted for her by Giovanni Bellini, he judges it in terms of its invention and coloring.[6] Cinquecento and seicento ekphrastic descriptions, which are almost always encomiastic, are critical not only because they imply or assume certain artistic values, such as naturalism and the expression of emotions, but because in them the writer often praises specific qualities of the work, such as proportion and decorum. Furthermore, ekphrastic descriptions are a form of criticism in the sense that the writer of them almost always interprets the subject matter of the work described.

Although there have been some excellent contributions to the study of ekphrasis as a way of writing about art, it yet stands in need of analysis, for it is often mistakenly viewed as little more than a literary device purloined from the poets and consequently subject to "serious limitations." Properly understood, however, the descriptions of Titian's painting not only give us an indispensable understanding of the work's *fortuna critica* — that is, its meaning and value for some of the finest writers about art in the Renaissance and Baroque periods — they also help us to reconstruct, at least to an extent, how people responded to that work, as well as to paintings in general.

Ernst H. Gombrich has said that most of Renaissance art criticism, which he defines as "the detailed assessment of both the merits and shortcomings of an individual work of art," is "disappointingly poor."[7] He is referring here specifically to ekphrasis or "poetic tribute," as he calls it, which repeats "the conventions evolved by ancient writers of epigrams." Gombrich, in effect, laments the fact that this particular kind of art criticism — which, as we have said, is almost uniformly encomiastic — does not do what it was not meant to do. In other words, ekphrasis is essentially evocative in nature, not analytical, and as evocation is often astonishingly successful. Gombrich also does not reveal that ekphrastic art criticism was not meant to assess merits and shortcomings.

[6] Lorenzo's letters are published in Brown and Lorenzoni, *Isabella d'Este*, 83–5, docs. 90, 92, 93. For a discussion of practical criticism, see Michael Baxandall, "Alberti and Cristoforo Landino: The Practical Criticism of Painting," in Accademia Nazionale dei Lincei, *Convegno internazionale indetto nel V centenario di Leone Battista Alberti* (Rome, 1974), 143–56.

[7] Ernst H. Gombrich, "The Leaven of Criticism in Renaissance Art," in *Art, Science, and History in the Renaissance*, ed. Charles S. Singleton (Baltimore, 1967), 3.

Rather it conveys a particular response to, and experience of, art. In ekphrasis the viewer, while aware of the medium in which the work is made, nevertheless treats the representation as if it were nature itself. This ekphrastic response is imaginative and interpretative rather than rational and analytical.

Like Gombrich, André Chastel notices that ekphrastic description is conventional in nature; that is to say, its sources lie in the literature of Antiquity, from Homer to Lucian, to Achilles Tatius and beyond, from which it derived its conventions.[8] Again like Gombrich, Chastel maintains that poetic description has "serious limitations," but for a different reason. "Its documentary value," he writes, "has to be treated with care." This warning implies that ekphraseis are not precise records of works of art, which implication is correct, but it fails to consider that descriptions of works of art, including those discussed here, were not intended to be "objective" records. They are, in a sense, like Rota's print (plate 27), inasmuch as they do not faithfully mirror the colors of the original composition, nor do they record every detail of Titian's painting. For example, none of them mention the small figure on horseback in the lower right-hand corner, and except for Carlo Ridolfi (see chapter seven), none say that Saint Peter Martyr in the original inscribed with his finger in the earth beside him the words "Io credo in Dio omnipotente."[9] Indeed, the iconography of the painting is not discussed at all, except by Ridolfi. Those writers assumed that kind of knowledge on the viewer's part and did not feel the need to repeat it in their criticism. On the other hand, descriptions are documents of a sort, for they record one way in which critics responded to works of art and the kinds of value they placed on art within the context of that response.

Chastel also observes that ekphrasis "tends, in effect, to free the idea underlying the work of art"; it is not "the direct expression of a reaction to the work, but primarily an interpretation of its meaning." Chastel seems to mean that ekphrastic criticism interprets the subject matter of, say, a painting, rather than reacting to it as art. He

[8] André Chastel, "The Arts During the Renaissance," in *The Renaissance: Essays in Interpretation* (London and New York, 1982), 259. See also idem, "Roberto Longhi: Il genio dell'*ekphrasis*," in *L'arte di scrivere sull'arte: Roberto Longhi nella cultura del nostro tempo* (Rome, 1982), 63.

[9] For the legend surrounding this inscription, see Meilman, "Titian's Saint Peter Martyr," 236 note 76.

continues by explaining that the "contribution" of the work "exceeds what is said in the texts." In other words, ekphrasis is limited in what it can say about a painting, and critics "hardly ever tried to find a 'poetic equivalent' " for it. Whereas it is true that, like Dante, who saw the relief-sculptures and the scenes in the pavement of Purgatorio as expressions of humility and pride, respectively, those who wrote on Titian's painting (plate 27) saw it as an embodiment of the idea of martyrdom, which view is certainly interpretative. But at the same time those critics responded to the artful naturalism of the work, to its masterful coloring and to its powerful expression.

Chastel's comments on ekphrasis are related to those of Michael Baxandall, who has pointed out that the Renaissance critic's response to a work was to a large extent shaped by the conventions of his criticism. Because of the very nature of ekphrastic art criticism, writers were limited in the kinds of things they could say about a work of art. Ekphrasis was governed by literary conventions and developed "in the Renaissance beholder or describer an awareness and expectation of those characters most suitable for description." Critics, in other words, focused on those features of a work of art that offered "a basis for deployment of available literary skills."[10] This is particularly true of fifteenth-century critics recently discussed by Baxandall, but by mid-sixteenth century, art criticism was informed not only by literary conventions but by an understanding of artistic process as well. Furthermore, the literary topoi employed by these critics serve to call attention to elements of the creative process. For instance, in his discussion of *colorito*, Dolce matches the lifelike appearance of good coloring and a variation on a topos common in the Renaissance, "it only lacks a voice" — the figures in a well-colored painting, he says, will "only lack breath."[11] Thus, as we shall see later on, the Petrarchan "brow" in Aretino's description of the *Saint Peter Martyr* and the reference to the speaking figure in Dolce's are tokens for Titian's powers of invention on the one hand and his naturalistic coloring on the other.

Chastel and Baxandall seem to be imposing limitations upon ekphrasis that were not perceived in the Renaissance. If today we see aspects of Titian's paintings that are not evoked in ekphrasis, it

[10] Michael Baxandall, "Guarino, Pisanello and Manuel Chrysoloras," *Journal of the Warburg and Courtauld Institiutes* 28 (1965):192.

[11] Lodovico Dolce, *Dialogo della pittura*, in *Trattati*, 204.

means only that we view his art differently from his contemporaries. For instance, although earlier critics certainly attended to
Titian's brushstroke in a variety of ways, we, who live in a post Abstract Expressionist era, may be better able to analyze that facet of
his art than they were, but we are less able to respond to the naturalistic illusion in his paintings, chiefly because we no longer place
much value on that aspect of his art. Indeed, we may find a "poetic
equivalent" for the expressiveness of Titian's brushstroke, whereas
his contemporaries could not, but Aretino's description is certainly
a poetic evocation of the powerful effect Titian's naturalism had
upon the sixteenth-century viewer.

In a more recent discussion of ekphrasis, David Carrier contrasts
it with modern art historical interpretation. He says that ekphrasis,
"tells the story represented, only incidentally describing pictorial
composition," whereas an interpretation "gives a systematic analysis of composition." Carrier also says that evocative description is
"not concerned with visual precedents," in contrast to interpretations which "explain how inherited schema are modified," and
ekphrasis, he continues, "only selectively indicates details," but interpretation "attends to seemingly small points which may, indeed,
change how we see the picture as a whole when they are analyzed."
Furthermore, "an interpretation treats the picture as an image, and
so tells both what is represented [as in ekphrasis] and how it is
represented."[12] Carrier's definition of ekphrasis in relation to art
historical interpretation seems to be correct, except that, contrary to
what he says, description does interpret the painting within the context of its subject matter. Nevertheless, the mode of art historical
interpretation is different.

Carrier also holds that an earlier ekphrasis may be supplanted
by an interpretation. While one sees what he means, it is possible
to clarify the issue further. Suppose that an art historian were to offer a new, convincing interpretation of Titian's painting, as seen in
Rota's print (plate 27), or one of the other copies, based upon an
examination of the small figure on horseback in the distance just
behind the assassin's right leg, a detail none of the earlier critics
even mention. Suppose, too, that this explanation radically altered

[12] David Carrier, "Ekphrasis and Interpretation: Two Modes of Art History
Writing," *British Journal of Aesthetics* 27 (1987): 20–21.

the way in which we see the work.[13] Would the new interpretation really supplant the earlier ekphraseis? We may answer that it would, indeed, take the place of the earlier descriptions *as an interpretation of the subject matter*, but the ekphraseis would still have value as examples of how their authors understood Titian's painting. Moreover, the descriptions would still be valuable evocations of the effect of the painting upon the viewer. Ekphraseis, in other words, have historical value, for they help us to see works of art, including Titian's paintings, as sixteenth- and seventeenth-century viewers saw them. They assist us, that is, in overcoming the limitations of our own, late-twentieth-century biases.

The first mention of Titian's painting appears in a letter of Pietro Aretino, who is not only one of the most engaging literary figures of the Italian Renaissance, but should be considered one of its two most advanced critics, the other being his friend Giorgio Vasari. Aretino is widely known as the author of erotic books, pornographic poems and political lampoons, but he also wrote religious works, such as *La humanità di Christo*, first published in 1535 in Venice where he resided from 1527 until his death in 1556. For students of art literature, however, Aretino's most important work is his *Lettere*, which appeared in six volumes between 1537 and 1557 and contains over six hundred letters about art or artists.[14]

In a letter of 1537, addressed to Niccolò di Raffaello Pericoli, a Florentine sculptor and architect known as Il Tribolo (1500–1558), Aretino relates a meeting between himself and the architect, Sebastiano Serlio in which the latter described a Pietà that Tribolo was then carving in the writer's honor. As Serlio was speaking, Titian approached, and Aretino recounted to him how Tribolo, who thought the *Saint Peter Martyr* the most beautiful painting in all of Italy, and his friend, Benvenuto Cellini (1500–1571), also a sculptor, had responded to the picture when they saw it during a visit to Venice in 1535. Aretino writes that the painting turned Tribolo

---

[13] Other copies of the painting suggest that there were two small figures in Titian's original — one running, the other on horseback. The assassin, Carino, was accompanied by two men who fled before the murder took place. I am very grateful to Patricia Meilman for this observation.

[14] See Pietro Aretino, *Lettere sull'arte*, ed. Ettore Camesasca with commentary by Fidenzio Pertile, 3 vols. (Milan, 1957-1960). (Hereafter cited as *Lettere.*)

into the image of wonder; and the eyes of sight and the lights of the intellect fastened on that work, you understood all the living terrors of death and all the true sorrows of life in the brow and in the flesh of him who has fallen to the ground, marvelling at the coldness and the lividness that appear in the tip of his nose and in the extremities of his body; and not being able to restrain your voice, you let loose a cry, when in the contemplation of the companion who flees, you discerned in his appearance the whiteness of cowardice and the pallor of fear...What a marvelous group of infants is in the air, standing out among the trees, which spread out their branches and leaves; what a landscape captured in its natural simplicity; what mossy stones bathed by the water that flows from the spring of the divine Titian's brush.[15]

This description and others like it scattered throughout the *Lettere* serve a number of purposes. They demonstrate Aretino's ability to write ekphraseis; they exhibit his knowledge of painting and its ends; they show him to be a friend and confidant of great artists; and they provide a kind of publicity for those artists as well as lesser ones. Moreover, like the descriptions in the *Imagines* of the elder Philostratus, they teach the reader how to respond to works of art. In the case of the letter about the *Saint Peter Martyr*, Tribolo's response to the painting, which is similar to that of Aretino himself in other letters, is an example of how it should be seen.

Aretino may also be making subtle allusion to two topics that were very popular in the sixteenth century, one, the *paragone* of sculpture and painting, which was essentially an argument about which of the two arts is superior, and the other, the comparison of visual images and verbal ones. Because Aretino has two sculptors respond so enthusiastically to Titian's painting, he implies the power of two dimensional images to move deeply artists who were accustomed to working in three dimensions. Moreover, his own reaction to Serlio's description of Tribolo's sculpture is rather restrained compared to the way in which the two sculptors respond to Titian's painting. Aretino implies here, perhaps unconsciously, the superiority of visual images over the written or spoken word. In other words, Titian's visual image moves Tribolo and Cellini more profoundly than the words of Serlio move Aretino.

---

[15] For the relevant text of Aretino's letter, see Appendix B, 1.

Another subject of the letter to Tribolo is ekphrasis itself, for just as Serlio's evocation of certain qualities of the sculptor's *Pietà* made Aretino see "the afflictions of the Virgin and the misery of her son" in his mind's eye even before he had seen the actual sculpture, his own description of Tribolo's response to the *Saint Peter Martyr* evokes certain qualities of the painting in the mind of the reader of his letter.

The evocative nature of ekphrasis may be most clearly seen, perhaps, when Aretino's description is compared with that of Raffaello Borghini of the same painting:

> In the church of Santi Giovanni e Paolo, [is] the painting on the altar of Saint Peter Martyr, where is the said saint larger than life in a wood of very large trees, fallen to the ground and wounded in the head by a soldier, so that one knows him to be on the point of death, with another figure; and in the air [are] two nude angels, who descend from a light in the sky, which illuminates the landscape, and this painting is the best conceived and executed with the greatest diligence that Titian ever made.[16]

Borghini, who relies on Vasari's ekphrasis of the same painting (see below), provides an example of almost pure description, for he limits his praise to the painting's conception (or invention) and the artist's diligent execution of it, but, unlike Aretino, makes no attempt to evoke any other aspects of the work, nor to interpret the scene before him, except where he says that the saint's wound signals his proximity to death.

Aretino's description, on the other hand, records his response to the work of art, although he conveys it through that of another. His account of Tribolo's reaction to Titian's painting has two facets, one having to do with "the eyes of sight" and the other with "the lights of the intellect." In the first instance, Aretino is referring to Titian's powerful illusion of nature. The artist, he implies, is like God insofar as he creates with his brush a world that, like the real world, is capable of astonishing its viewer with such qualities as the coldness and lividness of the visible flesh of the fallen saint, who is close to death. Tribolo's response also involves understanding, "the lights of the intellect." When Aretino writes that the sculptor

16 For the text of Borghini's description, see Appendix B, 2.

"understood all the true terrors of death and all the true sorrows of life in the brow" of the saint, he is referring to this internal vision. His reference to the saint's brow has its origin in a well-known line by Petrarch: "Ma spesso ne la fronte il cor si legge" (sonnet ccxxii: "But often one may read the heart in the brow"). In other words, as Renaissance art theorists often explained, the gestures and facial expression of a figure reveal its internal state. By such means, Tribolo was able to "read" the emotions of the saint and to see the cowardice and fear of his companion. We should note, too, that color is a means of expression as well, for the lividness of the saint's flesh expresses his inner state, as does the whiteness of that of his companion.

The last line of Aretino's description is crucial to an understanding of his, or Tribolo's, response to the painting. He says that the mossy stones are bathed by the water that flows from Titian's brush. In other words, Titian has created an illusion of nature to which Tribolo reacts as if it were real. The viewer, then, knows that he is looking at a representation in paint, yet views it as if it were actually happening.[17] He gives "imaginative assent" to the pictorial fiction, consciously suspending his awareness of the medium in order to respond imaginatively to the naturalistic depiction. Aretino's response, it should be noted, is not essentially new; its various elements had been embodied in ekphrastic descriptions of art since the *Imagines* of the elder Philostratus.

Aretino's description of Titian's *Saint Peter Martyr* (plate 27) is primarily an evocation of the painting's naturalism, especially in the expression of emotions, which are injected into the figures by the viewer within the context of the picture's subject matter. We must assume that the subject matter was known to Tribolo, for Aretino assumes it to be known to the reader of his letter. In short, Tribolo's response and that of Aretino are primarily aesthetic, and the religious dimension of the painting is assumed. At other times, however, Aretino responded quite differently to Titian's religious paintings. For instance, in his description of another of the artist's works, an unidentified *Ecce Homo* (perhaps like the one in Saint Louis; plate 28), actually a copy of a painting sent to the Emperor

---

[17] For an explanation of the psychological basis of the Renaissance response to art, see Norman E. Land, "Ekphrasis and Imagination: Some Observations on Pietro Aretino's Art Criticism," *Art Bulletin* 68 (1986): 209–12. See also David Summers, *The Judgment of Sense: Renaissance Naturalism and the Rise of Aesthetics* (Cambridge, 1987), 126–7.

Charles V, he writes of the figure of Christ:

> Of [real] thorns is the crown that wounds him, and the blood
> that their points cause him to shed is [real] blood. In no other
> way can the scourge swell and make livid the flesh than that
> in which your divine brush has made livid and swollen the
> immortal limbs of the sacred image; the sorrow that grips
> the figure of Christ moves to penitence anyone who views
> as a Christian his arms cut by the rope that binds his hands.
> He who contemplates the wretched deed of the cane which
> he holds in his left hand learns humility; and he who
> perceives the peaceful grace that his face shows forth has not
> the boldness to hold in himself a speck of hate and rancor.
> Thus, this [my] place for sleep no longer seems a courtly and
> worldly room, but a holy temple of God.18

Aretino first praises the naturalism of Titian's figure — the
wounds that look like real wounds and the blood that looks like
actual blood. He then says that if one views the painting as a
Christian, one will be moved to penitence and that one will be
moved to humility in the contemplation of the cane that Christ
holds and its significance. Moreover, the peaceful expression of
Christ's face (a product of Titian's skill) will purge the viewer of
hate and rancor. Aretino's response, then, is Christian insofar as he
views Titian's skill in relation to the subject matter of his painting
and its religious significance. For him, the *Ecce Homo* is not only a
beautiful example of Titian's stupendous ability, it is a religious
work that moves the viewer who sees it from a Christian point of
view to feel what those who are not sympathetic to the subject matter would not feel. Indeed, Aretino seems to suggest that the *Ecce
Homo* transforms the viewer from a worldly connoisseur into a
Christian beholder, just as the powerful painting seemed to change

---

18 Aretino, *Lettere*, 2:191: "Di spine è la corona che lo trafigge, ed è sangue il
sangue che le lor punte gli fanno versare; né altrimenti il flagello può enfiare e
far livide le carni, che se l'abbia fatte livide ed enfiate il pennello vostro
divino ne le immortali membra de la divota imagine; il dolore, in cui si ristrin-
ge la di Gesù figura, commuove a pentirsi qualunque cristianamente gli mira
le braccia recise de la corda, che gli lega le mani; impara a essere umile che
contempla l'atto miserrimo de la canna la quale sostiene in la destra; né
ardisce di tenere in sé punto di odio e rancore colui che scorge la pacifica
grazia che in la sembianza dimostra. Tal che il luogo u' dormo non par più
camera signorile e mondana, ma tempio sacro e di Dio."

his bedroom into a sacred temple.

Aretino's description of the *Ecce Homo* and his response to it are related to his criticism of Michelangelo's *Last Judgment* on the altar-wall of the Sistine Chapel (plate 26), as found in a letter of November 1545 to the artist.[19] He is dismayed by Michelangelo's representation of nudes whose postures he finds irreverent and whose genitalia are not covered. This latter circumstance especially, he argues, is indecent and more appropriate to a brothel than to such a holy place as the Chapel. The operative critical concept in this criticism is that of decorum or *convenevolezza*, to use Dolce's term. According to Aretino, Michelangelo should have given his figures more suitable postures and should have covered the offensive parts of his figures' anatomies so that they would not be inappropriate to the sacred place in which they appear.

Aretino praises the "vivacità del disegno" ("liveliness of the design") in the *Last Judgment*, but also says that Michelangelo, a Christian, has more regard for his art than for his faith ("più stimare l'arte che la fede"). Beauty for the sake of beauty is unacceptable in such a work, and Aretino recalls the example of Pope Gregory the Great, who tore down the pagan statues of Rome so that their beauty would not turn reverence away from the humble images of the saints: "Gregorio, il quale volse inprima disornar Roma de le superbe statue degli Idoli, che torre bontà loro la riverentia a l'humili imagini de i santi." Because Michelangelo had misused his skills as an artist, his painting is like those distracting ancient sculptures, and the viewer cannot properly respond to it; that is, he cannot respond "cristianamente." This view is perfectly consistent with that which Aretino expounded about Titian's *Ecce Homo*, in which beauty and skill are in the service of Christian subject matter.

As one scholar has pointed out, Aretino "attributes immense rhetorical power" to Titian's *Saint Peter Martyr*.[20] The expression of terror, fear, and cowardice by the figures caused Tribolo to cry out as if the actual martyrdom were taking place before his eyes. This emphasis upon the painting's rhetorical power and overwhelming illusion is also present in Lodovico Dolce's description of the paint-

[19] Letter to Michelangelo published by Gaye and Reumont, *Carteggio inedito*, 332–5.

[20] Lora A. Palladino, "Pietro Aretino: Orator and Art Theorist," (Ph.D. Diss., Yale University, 1981), 140.

ing.

Dolce, a Venetian humanist, who was acquainted with Aretino and served as an editor of his *Lettere,* has one of the two interlocutors of his dialogue, the figure of Pietro Aretino, describe the work to the other, a fictionalized Tuscan scholar named Giovanni Francesco Fabrini. Titian, he says,

> made the altarpiece depicting Saint Peter Martyr fallen to ground, with the assassin, who raises his arm to strike him, and a friar, who flees, with some small angels in the air, who are descending, as with the crown of martyrdom, and a landscape with some bushes and elder trees; all of which things are of such perfection that they can sooner be envied than imitated. He shows the friar in flight with a face full of fright; and it seems that one hears a cry and his movement is very vigorous, like that of one who is afraid for good reason, not to mention that his drapery is made in a manner which [in the works of] others one does not see an example. The face of Saint Peter contains the pallor that the faces of those close to death have, and the saint thrusts forward an arm and a hand of such merit that it may well be said that Nature has been conquered by Art. I will not go on to narrate the beauties of the invention, the design and the coloring, for they are known to you and to everyone.[21]

At first glance, Dolce's description seems to be merely an echo of Aretino's, which he certainly knew, but in fact it is organized in a significantly different manner, one that is related to Dolce's theory of artistic process.

According to Dolce, the art of painting is divided into three parts — *inventione, disegno,* and *colorito.* Invention, he says, "comes from two parts: from the *istoria* and from the talent of the painter" ("vien da due parti: dalla istoria e dall'ingegno del pittore"), and adds that "from the *istoria* he has simply the material and from his talent, other than the disposition and decorum, proceed the attitudes, the variety and the (so to speak) *energia* of the figures, but this is common to design" ("dalla istoria egli ha semplicemente la materia, e dall'ingegno, oltre all'ordine e la convenevolezza, procedono l'attitudini, la varietà e la [per così dire]

---

[21] For the text of Dolce's description, see Appendix B, 3.

energia delle figure; ma questa è parte comune dal disegno").[22] *Disegno* or drawing has to do with proportion, which is its "principal fondamento," variety, and movement, the last of which is "amazing," for it "amazes the eyes of the viewers to see in stone, on canvas or in wood an inanimate thing that appears to move" ("fa stupir gli occhi de' riguardanti, vedere in sasso, in tela o in legno una cosa inanimata, che par che si mova").[23] *Colorito* or coloring has to do with the imitation of nature and is so important and compelling that, when "the painter imitates well the colors and softness of the flesh and the property of anything, he makes his picture seem alive, so that they lack nothing but breath" ("il pittore va imitando bene le tinte e la morbidezza delle carni e la proprietà di qualunque cosa, fa parer le sue pitture vive e tali che lor non manchi altro che 'l fiato").[24]

Dolce's description of Titian's painting is organized according to his understanding of this three-part process of invention, drawing and coloring. He first identifies the invention as the martyrdom of Saint Peter Martyr and then gives a general description of the disposition of the main figures and the landscape. Next, he calls attention to the "vigorous" movement of the fleeing friar and the forward-thrusting hand of the saint, and, at the same time, describes the variety of their expressions and the naturalism of Saint Peter's pallid coloring.

Dolce's ekphrasis, unlike Aretino's, occurs within the context of a treatise on art, his *Dialogo della Pittura* (Venice, 1557). Thus, his description of Titian's painting and others serve a different purpose, that of illustrating ideas expounded in his book. In other words the organization of his extended description of Raphael's lost watercolored cartoon of the coronation of Roxana is similar to that in his ekphrasis of the *Saint Peter Martyr*.[25] In the former, however, he is illustrating the point that Raphael is outstanding in invention, and so focuses on that aspect of the work, while in his discussion of Titian's work, he maintains that the artist is unsurpassed, not only in invention, but in drawing and coloring as well and so describes all three elements. Nevertheless, his response to

[22] Dolce, *Dialogo*, 171.

[23] Ibid., 180.

[24] Ibid., 183.

[25] Ibid., 191–2.

Raphael's work as a lifelike imitation of nature is essentially the same as that to Titian's painting.

There are important aspects of Dolce's description of the *Martyr-dom of Saint Peter Martyr* other than its underlying structure. For example, after describing the main compositional elements of the painting, he praises it as a thing of perfection that "can sooner be envied then imitated." The author here alludes to a well-known inscription by Zeuxis, who, according to Pliny (*Naturalis historiae*, xxxv, 63), wrote beneath a painting of an athlete, with which he was especially pleased: "invisurum aliquem facilius quam imitatu-rum."[26] Dolce here indirectly praises Titian by associating him with the ancient artist; Titian, he implies, is the equal of the ancient artist. Dolce also says that the fleeing friar seems to cry out. This is a conventional way of praising an artist's ability to imitate nature, but it also conveys Dolce's imaginative participation in Titian's painting.

Like Aretino, Dolce admires the rhetorical expression of Titian's work, but unlike the former, he emphasizes its resemblance to nature and gives a somewhat different interpretation to the dramatic action of the fleeing friar. Aretino attributes the friar's movement to cowardice, whereas Dolce holds that his vigorous movement away from the saint is like that of an actual person confronted with the same circumstances, who "for good reason" would also flee. Moreover, the pallor of the saint's face, he says, comparing Titian's figure to nature, is like that of an actual person who is close to death.

Like Aretino and Dolce, Giorgio Vasari emphasizes the rhetori-cal power of Titian's painting, recognizing as he does so the artist's ability to make his figures appear to be alive. Focusing the reader's attention on the dramatic relation among the main figures, he writes that Titian executed

the painting on the altar of Saint Peter Martyr in the church of Santi Giovanni e Paolo, representing there the said holy martyr larger than life in a wood of very large trees, fallen to the ground and ferociously attacked by a soldier, who has wounded him in the head, and since he is half-alive, one sees in his face the horror of death; while in the friar, who

[26] *The Elder Pliny's Chapters on the History of Art*, trans. K. Jex-Blake, (Chi-cago, 1968), 108: "Another may envy more easily than he may imitate."

flees forward, one perceives the fright and dread of death: in the air are two nude angels, who come from a light in the sky, illuminating the landscape, which is very beautiful, as is the whole work; [this painting] is the most complete, the most celebrated and greater and better understood than any other that Titian has yet made in all of his life.[27]

Vasari calls attention to some of the same elements that Dolce does. He describes the invention, in both senses of the term, and the variety of the expressions. He does not refer directly to the coloring, as Dolce and Aretino do, but neither of them describe the emotional state of the saint's assassin. Vasari refers to his *fierezza*, his ferocity or fury, and thereby enhances the reader's understanding of the psychological complexity of Titian's scene. Indeed, Vasari distinguishes three kinds of fear in the saint and his companion as they react to the murderous soldier. The martyr's face shows the horror ("orrore") of death, while the friar exhibits dread ("timore") and fright ("spavento").

Vasari's evocation of the artist's dramatic portrayal of the saint's martyrdom does not specifically mention the artist's powers of imitation, but this is certainly due to the context in which the description appears, Titian's *Vita*. The general thrust of Vasari's biography of the artist is that Titian is an unequalled colorist, that the artist is supreme in the lifelike representation of nature, but is lacking in *disegno*. The fact that Vasari is able to invest distinct emotions in Titian's figures, then, is vivid testimony to their semblance to nature — they are like real people.

In his description of the *Saint Peter Martyr*, Vasari assumes the painting's religious content, but he is capable of viewing Titian's works "cristianamente," to use Aretino's word. For instance, he writes of one of the artist's pictures of the penitent Mary Magdalene, which was perhaps similar to the one in the Palazzo Pitti (plate 29), as follows: "Afterwards Titian made...a figure [shown] from the mid-thigh upward, of a dishevelled Saint Mary Magdalene; that is, with hair that falls over her shoulders, around her throat, and over her breasts, while she, raising her head with a gaze fixed heavenward, reveals compunction in the redness of her eyes,

---

27 For the text of Vasari's description, see Appendix B, 4. For an excellent discussion of Vasari's use of ekphrasis, see Svetlana Leontief Alpers, "Ekphrasis and Aesthetic Attitudes in Vasari's *Lives*," *Journal of the Warburg and Courtauld Institutes* 23 (1960): 190–215.

and in her tears sorrow for her sins." Vasari goes on to provide what is really a comment on his own description. He says that "this picture moves extremely anyone who sees it" ("muove questa pittura, chiunche la guarda, estremamente"), and that although the figure is very beautiful, "it moves not to lust but to compassion" ("non muove a lascivia, ma a comiserazione"). Just as the Magdalene is shown to be triumphant over her venal sins, so too does the figure triumph over the viewer's carnal desires and moves him to compassion, to a religious response.[28] Her gesture and expression, products of Titian's skill, and their significance make the viewer see her within the context of her identity, rather than as simply a beautiful female nude sensually wrapped in her own hair.[29]

In addition to describing the effect of Titian's *Magdalene*, Vasari also pays tribute to a particular aspect of the artist's character, as well as implicitly argue against Aretino's criticism of Michelangelo's *Last Judgment*. As he explains in his *Vita* of Fra Angelico, artists who paint religious works should themselves be religious, "being that one sees, when those things [i.e., works of art] are carried out by persons who have little belief in and little esteem for religion, that they often bring to mind impure appetites and lascivious desires, so that the work is blamed for its impurity and praised for its artifice and skill."[30] Vasari goes on to remark that ill-painted works are not necessarily devout, and that beautiful and good works are not necessarily lascivious just because they contain unusually attractive figures. His response to the painting of the Magdalene, then, conveys the idea that Titian has faith and regard for his religion, for his figure moves the viewer not to lust but to compassion. If viewers do see paintings like Titian's or, by implication, like Michelangelo's *Last Judgment*, as lascivious, they reveal the corrupt state of their own minds, as Vasari implies

---

[28] Vasari-Milanesi, 7:454: "Dopo fece Tiziano, per mandare al re Cattolico, una figura da mezza coscia in su d'una Santa Maria Maddalena scapigliata, cioè con i capelli che le cascano sopra le spalle, introno alla gola e sopra il petto; mentre ella, alzando la testa con gli occhi fissi al cielo, mostra compunzione nel rossore degli occhi, e nelle lacrime dogliezza de' peccati."

[29] Cf. Alpers, "Ekphrasis and Aesthetic Attitudes," 196.

[30] Vasari-Milanesi, 2:518: "...essendo che si vede, quando cotali cose sono operate da persone che poco credono e poco stimano la religione, che spesso fanno cadere in mente appetiti disonesti, e voglie lascive: ondo nasce il biasimo dell'opere nel disonesto, e la lode nell'artificio e nella virtù."

Aretino did, because they find impure intentions where there are none.

Aretino makes the distinction between the connoisseur's view of painting and that of the religious beholder, and, according to him, the latter's response to religious paintings is determined by the manner in which the artist has depicted his subject matter. Vasari agrees with Aretino but makes some further distinctions. In addition to the connoisseur, Vasari implies two different kinds of viewers, the worldly and the religious. Religious paintings by unfaithful and licentious artists will always be viewed as such, but presumably with approval by the worldly viewer and disapproval by the religious. If works created with no impure intentions are seen as "lascivious" by either the worldly or the religious viewer, it is the fault of the evil character of each and not that of the painting. Whatever their differences, however, both Vasari and Aretino were capable of seeing and describing the *Saint Peter Martyr* as a sacred image, but neither did. Both assumed its content.

8: Critical Values — Seicento

ARETINO, DOLCE, AND VASARI all evoke the rhetorical power and convincing similitude of Titian's *Martyrdom of Saint Peter Martyr* (plate 27), and as they do so, interpret the dramatic action of the main figures. In the late sixteenth century, the Anonimo del Tizianello, who may have been Giovanni Mario Verdizotti, a friend of the artist, wrote in a similar ekphrastic vein. In Titian's painting, he says,

> one sees Saint Peter Martyr who, wounded and fallen to the ground, reveals the sorrow and the affliction of the natural passions, and the discolored face of one who is struck down in a violent death; and one sees the friar, companion to the said saint and also wounded, so immersed in sorrow and desirous of saving himself that he naturally shows pallor in his face, the natural defense of his arm and flight in his feet; two angels of an infinite beauty, who descend from the sky, illuminate with visible splendor the darkness of the trees represented.[1]

For the Anonimo, the painting is not so much a scene of dramatic action, as it had been for Vasari; rather, it is primarily an expression of *dolore* (sorrow or grief). And, like Dolce, he compares the movements of the depicted figures to the natural actions of human beings as he assumes they would be in a similar situation. The pallor of the saint's companion is "natural" for one who is trying to save himself from death, as is his raised arm and his flight. Still, the stress here is not so much on Titian's ability to imitate nature faithfully, as was the case with Dolce, although that is assumed. Perhaps, again like Dolce, the writer was above all defending the

---

[1] For the text of the Anonimo's description, see Appendix B, 5. For Verdizotti, see Bernard Weinberg, *A History of Literary Criticism in the Italian Renaissance*, 2 vols. (Chicago, 1961), 2:330–2.

fleeing friar whom Aretino accused of acting out of cowardice.

The author's concern for the meaning of the subject is also suggested in his description of the two angels, who descend from the
sky as they bring the palm of martyrdom to the saint and illuminate the landscape. Dolce alludes to their significance in relation to
the saint (they bring the sign of martyrdom), and Vasari mentions
the light surrounding them, but the Anonimo's choice of
contrasting details — the light of the angels and the obscurity of the
trees — suggests a poetic analogy. The infinite beauty of the angels
and the light of heaven shining on the dark woods, he seems to
imply, together might be seen as an analogue of the divine illumination of the dark assassination of Saint Peter Martyr. In other
words, the evil darkness of the "natural passions" is expelled by the
light of heaven.

In the seventeenth century, Titian's famous altarpiece continued to receive attention from, among other critics and historians,
Carlo Ridolfi, Francesco Scannelli (1616–1663), and Luigi Scaramuccia (1616–1680).

Unlike previous writers, who seem to have assumed that the
viewer of the painting (plate 27) would already know the circumstances of its subject matter, Ridolfi, who was both a Venetian and
a painter, prefaces his description, in the manner of the elder
Philostratus, by recounting the incident that the picture represents:
"There appears in this [painting] the saint, who, returning to his
convent in Como (after having preached with great efficacy in
Milan against the wicked heretic), was mortally wounded by a cruel
highwayman, [who had been] roused by the heretics."[2]

Ridolfi then goes on at length to describe and to interpret the
action of the painting within the context of the subject matter. As
he does that, he emphasizes more than his predecessors had the details of the composition, although it is clear that he recalls the
ekphraseis of Dolce and Vasari.

> The event is represented chiefly in a thick wood of aged oak
> and other fully developed trees, which form with their bran-
> ches a shady screen as shelter from the sun. There the saint,
> fallen to the ground, is overcome by the pitiless murderer,
> who, grasping him by the edge of the cloak, fiercely repeats

---

[2] For the text of Ridolfi's description, see Appendix B, 6. Saint Peter was returning to Milan from Como.

his blow, while the glorious martyr, dipping his finger in his own blood, writes in the earth, even as he dies, "Io credo in Dio Padre omnipotente," authenticating even to the end the Christian faith. Meanwhile, his frightened companion, also wounded in the head, tries to save himself by fleeing, because the fear of death makes him abandon his friend in this moment of great need. Fear stands out on the saint's pallid face and heavy breathing seems to issue from his mouth, and because the torments would be unbearable, mercy on human frailty, if divine grace did not administer assistance by giving us a glimpse of future glory, two charming angels, descending from a celestial splendor, bring the generous martyr the palm of triumph, prepared for him in Heaven.

After this consideration of the work as an illusionistic representation of an historical event, Ridolfi discusses it as a work of art, never, however, losing sight of the subject matter. The angels, he explains, imitate a sculpture of cupids, said to be the work of Phidias. Thus, Ridolfi continues, Vasari is certainly mistaken when he writes that Titian did not study the art of Antiquity. The point here is that, just as Dolce had held and contrary to what Vasari says, Titian was accomplished in *disegno*. Furthermore, in this painting, Ridolfi asserts, Titian shows forth the greatest proof of his talent ("virtù") in the harmonious arrangement of the composition and the incomparable color, which is true to nature. He then turns to other features of the painting.

Consider the figure of the holy martyr in whose face one admires the pallors of death, or the ferocity of the barbarous murderer, [which figure is] no less learned in the understanding of the parts than in the placement of the muscles, or in the effects of the fear of the fugitive companion, which gives the impression, as one enters the church, of seeing a natural fact and the actual site of the woods, where in the distance on the summits of the mountains (as Dawn's white and vermilion disappear) the sun begins to rise little by little, gilding the azure sky with gold streaks, having taken as appropriate that [view] seen from the mountains of the Cenedese, which he saw from his own house. In conclusion, this most esteemed painting is reputed by every connoisseur to be the best of the artist's works, and in it he touched the most

sublime apex of art; so that one can reasonably write under it
that which Zeuxis said of his Athlete, his famous,
"Chi la invidii ben sia, non che'l imiti."

Here Ridolfi returns to the two main figures in Titian's composition, but now admiring them as examples of the artist's skill
rather than as actors in a religious drama. He also praises the landscape for its naturalism and evokes its qualities as such rather than
as a setting for the depicted martyrdom. In this last instance, he echoes Giovanni Paolo Lomazzo, who praised Titian's landscape, saying that it was "the most beautiful ever painted" ("il piú bello che
giamai fosse dipinto"), but without mentioning the figures in it.[3]
In other words, by the end of the sixteenth century, Titian's landscape was sometimes admired for itself alone, without regard for
the scene in which it appears.

In a poem of 1553, Pietro Aretino says, recalling certain lines in
Horace's *Ars poetica* (347-365), that Titian "forms landscapes in relief so beautifully that one is astonished by them either from near
or at a distance" ("Forma paesi in rilievo si bello / Che ne stupisce
il d'appresso e il lontano").[4] Perhaps following Aretino's lead,
Vasari also speaks of distant and close-up views of Titian's paintings in his discussion of the artist's early and late styles. Titian's
early works, he says, "are done with a certain fineness and incredib-
le diligence and are to be seen from near and from a distance" ("son
condotte con una certa finezza e diligenza incredibile, e da essere
vedute da presso e da lontano"). His late works, on the other hand,
"are carried out with strokes drawn broadly and with blots and
smears [across the canvas], in such a manner that from near the
paintings cannot be seen, and from afar they appear perfect" ("condotte di colpi, tirate via di grosso e con macchie, di maniera che da
presso non si possano vedere, e di lontano appariscono perfette").
Vasari suggests that distance from one of Titian's late paintings is
required in order to see its naturalism and illusion. Indeed, he says
that Titian's later method "is judicious, beautiful and stupendous
because it makes his pictures seem alive" ("è giudizioso, bello e stu-

---

[3] Giovanni Paolo Lomazzo, *Scritti sulle arti*, ed. Roberto Paolo Ciardi, 2 vols.
(Florence, 1974), 2:410. Lomazzo does not describe the painting.

[4] Aretino, *Lettere*, 2:436–7.

pendo, perchè fa parere vive le pitture").[5] Ridolfi seems to be thinking of Vasari's discussion when he says that from a distance, as one enters the church, the scene seems to be a "natural fact."

Ridolfi sees Titian's painting as a depiction of a religious subject and as an artful production; that is to say, like his predecessors, he sees Titian's painting in essentially two ways, as a likeness and as a work of art. These different modes of viewing a work of art are implied in Aristotle's distinction between the two "beings" of a picture. A painting exists both in and of itself and as a representation of something else: "a picture painted on a panel is at once a picture and a likeness: that is, while one and the same, it is both of these, although the 'being' of both is not the same, and one may contemplate it either as a picture or a likeness."[6] Ridolfi first contemplates the painting as a representation of an historical event and then goes on to describe it as a work of art.

An excellent illustration of these two views of the painting is the different ways in which Ridolfi describes the saint. First, he evokes the ferocity of the scene represented when he says that the saint's pallid face expresses fear as he is attacked by the pitiless assassin, but in the latter part of his description he admires the pallor of death in the saint's coloring and the ferocious expression of his barbarous murderer as examples of Titian's skill as an artist. To an extent, Ridolfi implies a difference between the viewer as a Christian responding to a religious picture and the viewer as a connoisseur admiring an artifact, just as Aretino had in his response to Titian's *Ecce Homo*.

Critics prior to Ridolfi do not specifically emphasize the religious nature of Titian's painting. They assumed that viewers of the painting (or readers of their texts) would already know the story of Saint Peter Martyr and that the painting would have a religious significance for them. Rather, those critics emphasize the painting's naturalism, the dramatic actions and expressions of the figures and their effect upon the viewer. On the other hand, while Ridolfi surely admires the painting's naturalism and the drama of its figures, it is above all for him a religious work.

The same may be said for Giovanni Domenico Ottonelli and Pietro da Cortona, who wrote about the painting around the same

---

[5] Vasari-Milanesi, 7:452.

[6] *De memoria et reminiscentia* (450 b, 21-24), in *The Works of Aristotle*, trans. John Issac Beare, 3 vols. (Oxford, 1908), 3:16.

time as Ridolfi, but did not describe it. They argue that the best and most highly valued works of certain modern painters are those of a religious, rather than profane subject matter, and cite Titian's painting as an example: "If anyone says that Titian has gained great honor as a painter of bacchanals, they [i.e., artists who paint religious subjects] respond that he has obtained even greater honor among connoisseurs for his *Saint Peter Martyr*, which...[is a]...very beautiful thing" ("Che se alcuno dicesse, Titiano hà ottenuto grandissimo honore conducendo i Quadri de' Baccanali: rispondo, che maggior l'hà conseguito appresso gl'intendenti, facendo la Tavola di S. Pietro Martire, che...[è una]...cosa bellissima").[7] For Ottonelli and Pietro da Cortona, Titian's skill remains relatively constant whatever subject matter he is depicting, but his religious works are more worthy of praise by virtue of their iconographical content.

Ridolfi's description of Titian's painting seems to have been shaped by a number of elements. In addition to the conventions of ekphrasis, Vasari's and Dolce's descriptions are determining factors. Like Vasari, Ridolfi dwells on the fear of the saint and his fleeing companion and on the ferocity of the assassin. Like Dolce, he hears a sound issue forth from the painting, not the friar's cry, however, but, more appropriately, the heavy breathing of Saint Peter Martyr, who is the central figure in the narrative. Moreover, he echoes Dolce's allusion to the inscription that Zeuxis placed beneath his picture of an athlete, but makes the reference explicit.

In addition, Ridolfi's response to Titian's painting seems to have been to an extent influenced by the art of his own time, although he appears neither to have understood nor to have liked it.[8] In other words, in pointing out (or, perhaps, fabricating) the dying saint's inscription in the earth, written in his own blood, a detail not mentioned by his sixteenth-century predecessors, Ridolfi adds a poignant dimension to the painting apparently not present

---

[7] Giovanni Domenico Ottonelli and Pietro Berrettini (Pietro da Cortona, pseud.) *Trattato della pittura e scultura: uso e abuso loro* (Florence, 1652), 201–2.

[8] See Robert Enggass's introduction to Carlo Ridolfi, *The Life of Tintoretto*, trans. Catherine Enggass (University Park and London, 1984), 3. See also Julius von Schlosser, *La letteratura artistica* (Florence, 1977), 531–2, 559.

for them, but certainly present in contemporary art.[9] Unlike cinquecento authors, he sees the painting not so much as the dramatic representation of a tragic, human event, but as an example of the triumph of the Christian faith.

Francesco Scannelli of Forlì was a physician, who knew Il Guercino and other painters of the Bolognese school and acted as an agent for Francesco d'Este, Duke of Modena, a great collector of art. Scannelli's relatively lengthy description of Titian's painting, like those of Dolce, Aretino and Vasari, emphasizes its naturalism, but a naturalism of a particular kind.

One still finds in Venice in the church of the Dominican friars, called Santi Giovanni e Paolo, that very famous painting of the martyrdom of Saint Peter Martyr, a work surely of the most excellent beauty, which in any age could so show forth nature in its most vivid effects as supremely to express the truth. Here the story is carried to the eye so adequately that a truth so greatly exact horrifies the imposed-upon spectator. One sees the saint in the middle part, who, fiercely assailed by his ferocious persecutor, finds himself in a place as in fact abandoned. One sees already the extremities of the body lacking in spirit and warmth, the languid face and the horrors of imminent death, and the revelation of life only shows in the eyes, while with his supreme spirit fixed on Heaven. Already by this time, his body lost, his soul is conscious of being at such a point to see the benefits of eternal life, where two putti show themselves in the truest proportion and delicate beauty with the crown and palm in hand in order justly to recognize the great champion, who with extraordinary intrepidity is undergoing martyrdom and death for Christ and his holy faith. The aggressor appears in the act of delivering new blows to the head of the dying saint, and within sight of so horrendous a spectacle, one sees a little way off the companion in the first motion accompanied by the truest and appropriate action, who already confused by fright shows with his most lively cries to give himself up completely as prey to the desperate flight, at the same time carrying to the viewer unexpected effects no less of fear and horror than

[9] This would be true even if Ridolfi invented the detail of the inscription written in blood in Titian's painting, as he may well have done. For this, see Meilman, "Titian's St. Peter Martyr," 236–7.

of wonder and compassion.[10]

Like the sixteenth-century critics, Scannelli assumes that the viewer will already know the story of the saint's martyrdom, but, unlike theirs, his response is a fusion of aesthetic and religious contemplation. While evoking the horrendous scene before him and its imposing effect upon the viewer, he can also remark the "delicate beauty" and "truest proportion" of the putti, qualities which are not only manifestations of Titian's *virtù*, but also expressive of the angels' divine nature. Indeed, the entire description may be read either as a tribute to the artist's skill or as a response to a representation of a significant religious event. Certainly Scannelli suggests as much. He praises the painting for its effect upon the viewer, who is made to feel, empathetically, not only fear and horror, but also wonder and compassion. Only a scene depicted with great skill will have the power to achieve this kind and degree of effect, and only on a sympathetic viewer, that is, one receptive to its subject matter.

Scannelli's response to Titian's work is shaped by his views of painting as an art and of the effect of art on the beholder.[11] The "worthy end of praiseworthy painting," he says, is "beauty" ("bellezza") or "grace" ("gratia"). This beauty, which is a reflection of the "supremo lume," or divine light in the "particolare idea," consists of proportion, a "softness of colors" ("soavità de' colori"), and decorum, all carried out with an "easy and true naturalism" ("facile e vera naturalezza"). Because Scannelli believes beauty is "a means by which one progresses to the recognition of God" ("una via per cui si camina alla cognitione di Dio"), painting is a "cleanser and not a corrupter of the emotions" ("purgativa, e non corrottiva de gli affetti"). The chief aim of Scannelli's book is to praise Correggio and the Lombard school, but given his ideas about art and beauty, it is not hard to understand why Titian's painting had such a powerful effect upon him.

In the last part of his description Scannelli steps away from the painting to view it only as a work of art, to admire its landscape for its own sake and to praise what he sees as its idealized naturalism.

[All of these things are] maximally represented in a wood,

---

[10] For the text of Scannelli's description, see Appendix B, 7. For Scannelli, see Schlosser, *La letteratura artistica* (Florence, 1977), 463, 614–5.

[11] Scannelli, *Il microcosmo*, 107–8, 131, 360.

which shows an appropriately proportioned landscape of the most facile excellence and beautiful truth and, like an abstract of the greater perfection, makes known in the end every most worthy part that one could desire in a composition of the choicest naturalism, with invention, disposition, and attitudes, which depicted with care and supreme intelligence regarding color, shows as the major sign of the most beautiful truth that is offered among painted works of art. The heads, hands, and feet, as well as the entire nude bodies, no less of the aggressor than of the angels, reveal a particular idea of the truth excellently expressed. And to show that such a prodigious narrative brings, so to speak, shame to the same nature [that it represents] it is enough to conclude that in fact it is the most complete and best painting that the great Titian, true father of the truest naturalism, ever created with his most remarkable blending of colors.

For Scannelli, then, the style of Titian's painting — its sense of proportion, its idealized beauty, and its decorum — is an example of what he considers to be the best manner.

Luigi Pelegrini Scaramuccia, called Il Perugino, was a painter whose book records the travels of an art student named Girupeno (i. e., Perugino) and his companion, the Genio of Raphael, throughout Italy. In Venice their guide is Marco Boschini, who is one of the outstanding writers on Venetian art. Boschini leads them to see Titian's painting, which they begin to admire the moment they enter Santi Giovanni e Paolo. They praise, the narrator says, the overall composition ("grand'accordamento del tutto insieme") and the great judgment Titian showed in considering every distance of the viewer from the painting. From afar, the narrator explains, recalling Vasari's and perhaps Ridolfi's discussion of this subject, one perceives the lights and darks as a thoroughly ordered composition, whereas closer to the painting Girupeno and Genio observe

the lightness of the brushstroke, and the putti, in which the painted texture is like that of flesh, descending from heaven amidst the most radiant brightness, bringing, sweetly and brightly, the glorious palm of martyrdom to the holy saint. And they take great delight in the reflections of the same brilliance on the leaves of a large tree, which is marvelously situated at the head of a beautiful and charming landscape.

And the two foreigners remain completely edified by the concentration on the murderous scoundrel, who with the accompaniment of a brawny physique wonderfully expresses his cruelty in his face, and they do not think it amiss to conclude that this is one of the most beautiful paintings that ever issued forth from the valorous hand of the great master Titian.[12]

Although Scaramuccia expounds an art theory similar in its classicism to that of his contemporary, Giovanni Pietro Bellori, his book is, in effect, a series of critical judgments on specific works of art, and his response to Titian's painting is not to any great extent determined by his theory.[13]

Girupeno and Genio seek instruction from art, and they respond to Titian's painting as students of art. They are astounded by Titian's brushwork, by the way in which he imitates textures with impasto, by his landscape, by the focus of the composition on the assassin, and by the expression of cruelty on his face and in his body. In short, they are impressed by the way in which Titian has brought his talent to bear upon this particular subject matter. For them, the painting, when seen from a relatively short distance, expresses a contrast, as it seems to have for the Anonimo del Tizianello, but this time between the bright refulgence and the sweet putti in the upper portion and the brawny murderer on which the composition focuses the viewer's attention. Though Girupeno and Genio did not come to Santi Giovanni e Paolo to worship, at least not God, but to learn about Titian's art, the religious significance of the painting did not escape them.

In one respect, all of the descriptions of Titian's painting we have discussed here, save that of Borghini, contain a similar response. This response, which had been conventional in ekphrastic descriptions of art from the time of Philostratus the Elder onward, is to the illusionistic naturalism of the work. As Elizabeth Cropper has so concisely explained, each author, "writing always in the present...summon[s] up a vision of the painted scene as if it were really

---

[12] For the text of Scaramuccia's description, see Appendix B, 8.

[13] See Guido Guibbini in Luigi Scaramuccia, *Le finezze de' pennelli italiani ammirate e studiate da Girupeno sotto la scorta e disciplina del Genio di Raffaello d'Urbino* (1674: Reprint, Milan, 1965), 13. See also Schlosser, *La letteratura artistica*, 537–8, 557.

happening, periodically destroying his fiction, and consequently drawing attention to its power of illusion, by withdrawing from the pictorial space to comment on the artifice of the painter."[14] In other words, while aware that they are looking at a work of art, the critics nevertheless accept or affirm the illusion and respond to the scene as if it were real. Figures seem to cry out, to breathe, to move, and to have emotions. In this state of mind, one of imaginative assent, the critic interprets the represented figures.

The figures in Titian's painting are interpreted variously, but always within the context of the subject matter. For example, Aretino sees the friar's pallor as a sign of his cowardice, but Dolce and the Anonimo del Tizianello see the figure's flight as "natural," given the circumstances of the scene. Ridolfi, perhaps consciously taking a middle course between the two views, says that fear drives the friar to abandon his friend, whereas, similarly, Scannelli holds that he is so "confused" by fear that he succumbs to flight. Likewise, the assassin is described as ferocious (Vasari, Ridolfi and Scannelli), pitiless (Ridolfi) and barbarous (Ridolfi) and as a "murderous scoundrel" (Scaramuccia).

The interpretation of the figures in Titian's painting is selective in two ways. First, only certain figures are chosen for description. Neither Aretino, nor the Anonimo, for example, mention the assassin while all the other authors do, and no one mentions the figure on horseback located in the woods to the right in Rota's print (plate 27). Secondly, each writer chooses certain details of the figures for description. Among the writers who describe the assassin, Dolce says that he raises his arm; Vasari that he has already wounded the saint; Ridolfi that he grasps the saint's cloak; Scannelli that he attacks the saint; and Scaramuccia says nothing about the figure's action. Moreover, except for Ridolfi, none of the writers say that saint is writing in the earth with his finger, a detail that perhaps he invented as a way of heightening the viewer's (or reader's) sense of the picture's pathos.

The description of Titian's landscape and the significance given to it also change from description to description. Whereas Aretino praises its "natural simplicity" and notices the stream of water with its mossy stones at the bottom of the composition, Dolce and Vasari make only passing reference to it, mentioning its naturalism and

---

[14] Quoting Elizabeth Cropper, *The Ideal of Painting: Pietro Testa's Düsseldorf Notebook* (Princeton, 1984), 171. Cropper is describing method in Bellori's ekphraseis.

beauty, respectively. For the Anonimo the landscape's importance lies in the darkness of its trees as it is illuminated by the light of the descending angels. Ridolfi first describes how the branches of the trees form a shelter from the sun (which celestial body no one else mentions) and later, connecting the scene with a view from Titian's house at Cadore, evokes its splendid colors. Scannelli admires the proportion of the landscape as well as its "facile excellence" and beautiful naturalism. Being students of art, Scaramuccia's characters take delight in the reflections of light on the leaves of one of the large trees, which is positioned at the head of the "beautiful and charming landscape."

Just as the landscape and the figures and their actions are interpreted differently, so, too, does the meaning of the painting as a whole change from author to author and from century to century. Aretino concentrates on the painting's naturalism and expression and on the powerful effect these have on the viewer, Tribolo. The picture is seen as primarily a monument to Titian's overwhelming abilities as an artist. For Dolce, the work illustrates one argument of his treatise, that Titian is outstanding in invention, design and coloring. Vasari, who implies the painting's naturalism, focuses on the emotional states of the three principal figures. More so than for Aretino and Dolce, the painting is for him a depiction of an intense dramatic action. The Anonimo seems to see far less variation than Vasari in the expressions of the friar and saint, both of whom, he says, express sorrow. Also important for him is the way in which the angels illuminate the darkness of the trees.

Sixteenth-century critics assume the painting's religious subject matter and content. For them, with its figures expressing familiar emotions, the scene is understood primarily in human terms. In the first part of Ridolfi's description, the picture's religious content moves to the foreground. After briefly recounting the story of Saint Peter Martyr, Ridolfi describes the scene much as his predecessors had, but adds significant details, such as the saint's (alleged) inscription in the earth, which "authenticates" the Christian faith. Moreover, the two angels are ministers of "divine grace," and the palm of martyrdom they bear was prepared for the saint in heaven. Thus, the painting is seen less as a human drama, as in cinquecento criticism, and more as an interplay between the human and the divine, an interplay often observed in seicento art.

In the second part of his description Ridolfi, in part responding to Vasari's *Vita* of Titian, turns to the painting as an example of the artist's skills — his knowledge of musculature and his ability to create an illusion that seems actual from a distance. As we have noted, Aretino and Vasari were capable of responding to Titian's religious paintings from a specifically Christian point of view, but regard the *Saint Peter Martyr* as connoisseurs. Ridolfi, on the other hand, joins the response of the religious beholder to that of the connoisseur. For him, the meaning of the painting is determined by the particular vantage from which it is seen. The connoisseur sees it as a work of art, as a product of the artist's skills, while the religious beholder sees it primarily as a depiction of a significant Christian event and assumes the artist's skills.

Scannelli, like Ridolfi, views the painting as an interplay of the divine and the human. As he dies for Christ, the saint's spirit is fixed on heaven, and he sees already the benefits of eternal life. Unlike Ridolfi, however, Scannelli views the painting simultaneously as a connoisseur and as a religious beholder. As he tells of the significance of the event in the first part of his description, he also remarks the painting's naturalism, beauty and decorum. In the second part he drops the religious view and focuses on the work as a expression of the brand of ideal naturalism he championed. For Scannelli, Titian's painting is meaningful above all as a skillful work of art exhibiting certain qualities, a circumstance that should not be surprising, for the description appears in a treatise on art.

Context also impinges upon the meaning of the painting for Scaramuccia, who describes not his own response as such, but that of his two main characters, Girupeno and Genio. Being students of art, they naturally respond primarily to the painting as a work of art, to its harmonious composition, its brushwork, and the expressions of its figures. Religious content is assumed and the painting's religious significance alluded to only minimally.

Given the complexity and range of twentieth-century art criticism (including the critical history of art), perhaps it is not surprising that we should find ekphrastic description limited in what it can say about a work of art. Renaissance and Baroque critics, because they employ the conventions of ekphrasis, could say only certain things about a painting such as Titian's. Even so, any method of art criticism has its inherent limitations, as the recent dissatisfaction with formalism, standard iconographical studies, and now the deconstructionists readily demonstrates. Within the limitations of the genre (and it seems appropriate to speak here of a genre), however, critics were able to summon forth the amazing power and overwhelming beauty of Titian's painting, whether they viewed it "cristianamente" or as connoisseurs, and even today, when we can no longer see the actual work, we yet feel something of that lost power and beauty through their descriptions.

Within the limitations of ekphrastic art criticism, writers were also able to interpret works of art and the figures in them in various ways. These interpretations are an important facet of the rich and complex history of Titian's painting; indeed, they are inseparable from it. Furthermore, because the painting is viewed as a dramatic event, critics focus attention on its main characters and their actions rather than on less significant details. Unlike the criticism found in recent art historical practice, the earlier descriptions eloquently convey the essential meaning of the narrative. That may well be why the small figure on horseback is never mentioned: it seems to have been beneath the threshold of appropriate interpretation. The descriptions, lastly, also provide valuable insight into not only the picture's *fortuna critica* but also its vital presence as a work of supreme art over an extended period of time, as well as the effect of that presence on some of the best critics of the sixteenth and seventeenth centuries.

9: Noble Frames

NICOLAS POUSSIN'S DEBT to Venetian art at the beginning of his career, in such works as his *Martyrdom of Saint Erasmus* for Saint Peter's in Rome (plate 30), is widely recognized.[1] Not only are the strong diagonal thrust of the composition and the columns at the top of the picture drawn ultimately from such works as Titian's Pesaro *Madonna and Saints*, but the coloring and handling of the paint echo the Venetian manner. Even after he developed a style closer to that of Raphael, Poussin's interest in Venetian art remained active.[2] For example, his *Self-Portrait* in the Louvre, Paris (plate 31) recalls, in terms of both composition and expression, such paintings as Titian's *Portrait of a Bearded Man* in National Gallery of Art, London (plate 32). In addition, Poussin's attraction to *colore*, a fundamental feature of Venetian painting, remained strong long after he had virtually abandoned the painterly manner of his early works.

Poussin's interest in coloring is directly related to his desire for a certain kind of frame for his paintings, a desire that may be understood through a critical appreciation of his *Self-Portrait* (plate 31). In turn, the best approach to understanding that painting remains Giovanni Pietro Bellori's *Vita* of the artist, first published in Rome in 1672. Indeed, Bellori's interpretation of the picture is the foundation upon which rest our present understanding of it and, by extension, our understanding of the artist himself. Moreover, because Bellori, who was a close friend of the artist, regarded the painting primarily as a likeness of Poussin, his descriptions of the physical appearance and of the character and personality of the

[1] For a brilliant discussion of Poussin's early works, see Konrad Oberhuber, *Poussin: The Early Years in Rome* (New York, 1988).

[2] Ann Sutherland Harris, *Andrea Sacchi* (Princeton, 1977), 28. See also Cropper, *The Ideal of Painting*, 144–6.

painter provide an avenue to the painting's meaning.[3] This essay expands Bellori's interpretation of the *Self-Portrait* and calls attention to the significance of a particular aspect of Poussin's art that has been largely overlooked, his concern for properly designed and gilded frames for his pictures — a concern that he more than once expressed to one of his most important patrons, Paul Fréart de Chantelou.

In the *Self-Portrait*, the painter, represented in half-length, wearing a somber black gown, like that of a learned academic, has turned his body toward the viewer's right-hand side. His head is illuminated from the left by a strong light and is so turned that the figure faces the viewer, while his right hand rests on a small portfolio tied with a bright red ribbon. His face is ruddy, as if he has spent long hours out-of-doors, and the rims of his eye lids are red, as if he has been intensely looking at something for a long, long time. To the left of the artist is what appears to be the back of a chair covered with a red, brocaded cloth.

Behind the image of Poussin are four canvases stacked against the wall of a room, probably his studio. All of the canvases are framed, and the frames of the first three are very simple in design and are gilded with a dull gold-leaf. The first canvas, which has been uniformly covered with a dark gray paint, serves as the support for a golden inscription informing the viewer that the figure is the likeness of the artist, painter from Andelys, who is fifty-six years of age, in Rome, in the Jubilee year of 1650 (*Effigies Nicolai Poussini Andelyensis Pictoris. Anno Aetatis. 56. Romae Anno Iubilei. 1650*). To the left of the figure, in a small portion of the second canvas, appear the head and shoulders of a woman wearing a diadem in the center of which is a single eye. This woman is embraced by two muscular arms and strong hands extending into the picture from the left-hand edge. Of the third canvas we see only a small segment of the top portion of its frame, and the face of the fourth canvas has been turned to the wall.

In one description of Poussin, Bellori explains how the artist would extemporaneously, yet intelligently, expound upon the art

---

[3] Giovanni Pietro Bellori, *Le vite de' pittori, scultori e architetti moderni*, ed. Evelina Borea (Turin, 1976), 421–81. For additional bibliography on Poussin's *Self-Portrait*, see Mattias Winner, "Poussin's Selbstbildnis im Louvre als Kunsttheoretische Allegorie," *Römisches Jahrbuch für Kunstgeschichte*, 20 (1983): 449. See also David Carrier, *Poussin's Paintings: A Study in Art-Historical Methodology* (University Park, 1993), 1–26.

of painting.

> [He] often spoke about art and with such clarity about mat-
> ters that not only painters, but also other talented men, came
> to hear from his mouth the most beautiful explanations of
> painting, given not with the aim of teaching but as the occa-
> sion arose. Having read and observed much, he never spoke
> of anything about which he had not a satisfactory knowled-
> ge, and his words and ideas were so appropriate and well
> ordered that they did not seem improvised, but studiously
> thoughtout.[4]

Poussin's intelligent explanations of the art of painting find a parallel in his *Self-Portrait*, portions of which, as we shall see, seem to express symbolically some of the artist's ideas about the art and how it
should be displayed.

The painting may also be seen as a complex visual discourse on
the fundamental nature of illusion in art. In the painting, we are
engaged first of all by the illusion of the person of Poussin, seated
in a space that is enclosed and separated from the actual world
about it by the picture's frame. Set against this illusion is the first
canvas, which, because it is painted a uniformly flat gray color, signals that the "corporeal vitality" of the figure of the artist is not
"real" — it, too, is painted on a similar flat surface. In the next
canvas, which carries the figure of the crowned woman, we are
confronted by another illusory world of art, or more precisely, by an
illusion-within-an-illusion, one that enhances the illusory reality
of the figure of the artist. This enhancement occurs because the
illusory world of depicted reality is set against the seemingly "real"
world in which the figure of Poussin exists. Because we see only its
reverse side, the fourth painting makes us once again recall the de-
ceptive nature of art, for it reminds us of the actuality of wooden
stretcher and flat canvas, which together are the support on which
painted illusions are created.

The inscription to the right of Poussin not only names but also
locates him in time and space. It also functions in such a way that
it, too, may be seen as an expression of the artist's keen visual intelligence. The words and numbers floating on the surface of the
gray canvas might be seen as a "verbal equivalent" of the image of

---

4 Bellori, *Le vite*, 451.

the artist just next to them. The framed, gray canvas and the inscription together could then be seen as a kind of self-portrait in
which painted image has been replaced by a written description.
We should remember in this regard that Poussin, referring to his
Israelites Gathering Manna (Paris, Louvre), once advised Chantelou, who commissioned the *Self-Portrait*, to "read the story and the
painting in order to perceive if each thing is appropriate to the
subject" ("Lisez l'histoire et le tableau, afin de connaître si chaque
chose est appropriée au sujet").5 Although the *Self-Portrait* is not a
narrative scene, we, nevertheless, literally read the inscription as
we "read" Poussin's painted image of himself.

Conceivably, the artist may also have been thinking of the *paragone* of art and poetry so important to Renaissance artists, like
Leonardo da Vinci who refers to in his notebooks. There the Florentine artist challenges poets to write the word "God" next to a
painted image of the same so as to observe which people will worship. If Poussin was recalling Leonardo, or some other authority,
on this subject, the *Self-Portrait* may also attest to the superiority of
the visual image, as a representation of nature, over the written
word.

Bellori tells us that Poussin's learning extended beyond painting
to include knowledge of both the Latin and Italian languages. Other
examples of the artist's knowledge, he says, "are the figures he designed for Leonardo da Vinci's *Trattato della Pittura*, published
with his [Poussin's] drawings in Paris in 1651."6 The figure in the
Louvre painting (plate 31) confirms the authenticity of Bellori's
implied comparison of the learned Leonardo and the erudite Fren-
chman. The artist's observant, penetrating eyes — his "eruditos
oculos," to borrow a phrase from Franciscus Junius — and his air
of intelligence and self-possession convince us that Poussin was, indeed, a very knowledgeable and perceptive man. At the very least
we are convinced that this is the way in which the artist wanted
others to see him and the way in which he saw himself.

Bellori also describes Poussin's physical appearance:

he was a large man, well-proportioned in all parts of his

---

5 Pierre du Colombier, ed., *Lettres du Poussin* (Paris, 1929), 12.

6 Bellori, *Le vite*, 451. For a recent study of Poussin and Leonardo, see Elizabeth Cropper, "Poussin and Leonardo: Evidence from the Zaccolini MSS,"
Art Bulletin 62 (1980): 570–83.

body, and with a most rare temperament; there was a certain amount of olive-green in his coloring; and his black hair was to a large extent gray with age. His eyes had a certain amount of pale, sky-blue in them, and his pointed nose, and spacious brow gave his face a noble, yet modest, appearance."[7]

This description, which immediately precedes Bellori's discussion of the *Self-Portrait*, serves as a kind of verbal evocation or ekphrasis of the painting and perfectly suits its style and the expression of the figure. The critic subtly fuses Poussin's physical features and his elevated character, making the artist's outward appearance a mirror of his soul. And this synthesis of outward appearance and inner ideal precisely parallels the balance of truth to nature and idealization of form in the painter's likeness of himself.

Bellori sees the *Self-Portrait* as primarily a likeness of the character and appearance of Poussin, but he also explains the symbolic meaning of the woman wearing the crown in the second canvas. She personifies the art of painting, and the two hands embracing her represent the love of painting and the friendship of one of the artist's most important patrons, Chantelou, for whom the likeness was made.[8] Thus, the artist "expressed his praise and affection" for Chantelou, "who favored him for his noble inclinations."[9] The nobility of character in the figure of the painter is, then, as Bellori suggests, the very quality that Poussin's friend and patron admired in him.

Even today we can understand the appropriateness of Bellori's attention to those qualities of Poussin's character, for the modest nobility of the artist's face, which is enhanced by his bearing and by his severe, black gown, remind us, under the influence of the critic's descriptions of the painter, not only of the nobility of his profession but of the nobility of intellect and emotion that we encounter in his works. We sense, too, in the well-proportioned figure a largeness — at once physical, mental and spiritual — which serves as an analogue of the vision generally expressed in his art: his grand and morally measured view of humankind and

[7] Bellori, *Le vite*, 455.

[8] On the symbolism of friendship in Poussin's painting, see Oskar Bätschmann, *Nicolas Poussin: Dialectics of Painting*, trans. Marko Daniel (London, 1990), 47–9.

[9] Ibid.

their history.

Although Bellori quite rightly focuses our attention on the figure of Poussin, the secondary objects in the painting affect our sense of him. As Walter Friedlander observed, for instance, the "severe, abstract-geometrical background contrasts with the volume of the portrait bust, shown in its full, corporeal vitality."[10] Moreover, the geometrical stability of the canvases and their frames lends the figure a sense of movement and liveliness, and the frames, with their simple designs ultimately derived from the vocabulary of Ancient architecture, enhance our sense of the artist's modesty and nobility. We should notice, too, that the serious (though certainly not pompous) expression of the artist's face is in contrast with the gentle smile of the crowned woman, a contrast which makes us feel that Poussin may have been humorously, perhaps even ironically, commenting upon his own rather somber presentation of himself.

Bellori identifies the crowned woman as a personification of the art of painting. This identification has led to a great deal of discussion among scholars, for, as Donald Posner has pointed out, she does not have the attributes traditionally associated with painting, nor is painting ever shown with a one-eyed crown on her head.[11] Posner has demonstrated that the crown-with-an-eye appears on one of the figures in an illustration of perspective in the edition of Leonardo's treatise on painting mentioned earlier and therefore alludes to the intellectual nature of the art. Thus, Posner suggests, Poussin's figure of painting would certainly have reminded Chantelou that, as the artist explained in a now-famous letter on the "modes," the art of painting is a lofty and intellectual activity.[12]

Poussin's figure of painting may also express his understanding of how we see things in nature. In an undated letter to Sublet de Noyers, probably of 1642, he wrote,

> There are two ways of seeing objects, one is seeing them simply, and the other is considering them with attention. To

[10] Walter Friedlander, *Nicolas Poussin: A New Approach* (New York, n.d.), 172–3.

[11] Donald Posner, "The Picture of Painting in Poussin's Self-Portrait," in *Essays in the History of Art Presented to Rudolf Wittkower*, eds. Douglas Fraser, Howard Hibbard, and Milton J. Lewine (London, 1967), 200.

[12] Ibid., 202.

see simply is nothing other than receiving in the eye the form and resemblance of the thing seen. But to see an object with attention involves not only the simple and natural reception of the form in the eye, but the study of it with particular application, the means to a better perception of this same object. Thus, one can say that the simple aspect is a natural operation and that which I call "Prospect" is an office of reason, which depends on three things, knowledge of the eye, of the visual ray, and the distance of the eye from the object.[13]

Poussin considered the act of painting to be a fusion of simple, natural vision and "prospect" or perspective, and the figure in the Louvre picture (plate 31) may be seen to possess those two ways of seeing objects, one in her "natural" eyes, and the other in the eye of her crown.

Support for this interpretation comes from the illustration at the beginning of Bellori's *Vita* of Poussin (plate 33), in which the art of painting is presented in a notably similar way. There a female figure, most likely a personification of painting, points to a flat plane or slab on which are depicted in linear perspective the outlines of various geometrical shapes (a cube, a slender pyramid, and a three-dimensional, block-like triangle), representing, to use Poussin's term, "prospect." To the right of the figure, the words "lumen et umbra" are inscribed on the surface of a large cube which bears a massive cylinder. Because light and shadow have to do with the natural impression of a form (i.e., the way we physically see things), they correspond to what Poussin called the "simple aspect" of an object and to "natural vision." Painting, as the illustration seems to suggest, fuses or at least employs two kinds of sight — the one "natural" and the other geometrical. This point would not have been missed by attentive readers of Bellori's *Vita*, who surely would

---

[13] Colombier, *Lettres du Poussin*, 77: "...il y a deux manières de voir les objets, l'une en les voyant simplement, et l'autre en les considérant avec attention. Voir simplement n'est pas autre chose que recevoir naturellement dans l'oeil la forme at la resemblance da la chose vue. Mais voir un objet en le considérant, c'est qu'outre la simple et naturelle réception de la forme dans l'oeil, l'on cherche avec une application particliére, le moyen de bien connaître ce même objet: ainsi on peut direque le simple aspect est un opération naturelle, et que ce que je nome le Prospect est un office de raison, qui dépend de trois choses, savoir de l'oeil, du rayon visuel, et la distance de l'oeil à l'objet."

have recalled the illustration (plate 33) as they read the reference in the text to the personification of painting in the *Self-Portrait* in the Louvre.

As Posner suggests, the figure of painting in the *Self-Portrait* may have caused Chantelou to recall the intellectual difficulty of art. Other elements of the picture, specifically the frames around the canvases behind the artist, might have reminded Chantelou of another facet of painting, one that is related to Poussin's theory of vision, and one that he thought especially important.

In 1639, eleven years before the date in the *Self-Portrait*, Poussin sent his *Israelites Gathering Manna* to Chantelou, and in a letter, already mentioned, about the work gave his patron some advice about a suitable frame for it.

> When you receive your [painting], I beg you, if you find it good, to give it a bit of framing, because it needs it, so that in considering all its parts, the rays of the eye will be held in and not dispersed outwardly in receiving the species [of rays] from other objects nearby, which coming pell-mell with [the rays of] the things painted, confuses the light.[14]

Although Poussin's theory of vision is ultimately derived from medieval treatises on optics, it is clear that he is advising his patron that a frame gilded with dull gold will so separate the painting from the objects around it that everything in the picture will be visible to the viewer. In other words, the artist wants the light reflected by the surface of the painting to be separated from the light reflected by the objects around it; otherwise, the two kinds of light will be confused. The dull gold frame will prevent the confusion because it will reflect not a harsh light, as would a frame gilded with burnished gold, but a soft light "that gently blends with the colors [of the painting] without offending them."

Poussin's concern for the colors in his painting suggests that he regarded the instruments of his art (that is to say, brushes and pa-

---

14 Ibid., 11: "Quand vous aurez reçu le vôtre [painting], je vous supplie, si vous le trouvez bon, de l'orner d'un peu de corniche, car il en a besoin, afin que, en le considérant en toutes ses parties, les rayons de l'oeil soient retenus et non point épars au dehors, en recevant les espèces des autres objets voisins qui, venant pêle-mêle avec les choses dépentes, confondent la jour. Il serait fort à que ladite corniche fût dorée d'or mat tout simplement, car il s'unit très doucement avec les coleurs sans les offenser."

lette) as something more than "technical accessories" to purely intellectual activity.[15] Indeed, such concern suggests, as Elizabeth Cropper has demonstrated in another context, that Poussin can no longer be considered as having been "committed to *disegno* rather than *colore*."[16] That the artist held color to be an important element of painting may also be gathered from another of his self-portraits, the one of 1649, now in Berlin. In that picture the figure holds a book with the title *Lumine et Colore* on its spine.[17] The artists deep concern for color may also be observed in his "Observations on Painting," printed by Bellori as an appendix to his *Vita* of the artist.

These "observations" are actually notes taken by the artist from books he had read, but they, nevertheless, give us a good idea of what he considered to be important to his vision of painting as an art.[18] For instance, he was struck by a sentence in Torquato Tasso's *Discourses on the Heroic Poem* regarding color and jotted down a note that reads, "Colors in painting are almost allurements for persuading the eye, like the beauty of verses in poetry."[19] Poussin defined painting in a traditional way. "It is," he wrote, "an imitation made with lines and colors on any surface of all that is seen under the sun."[20] The sentence from Tasso, then, seems to refer to the conventional function of colors in the painter's imitation of nature; they "persuade" the eye inasmuch as they are necessary to the artist's creation of a lifelike illusion of things.

[15] Cf. Posner, "The Picture of Painting," 202.

[16] Cropper, "Poussin and Leonardo," 570.

[17] For a discussion of this painting in relation to Poussin's *colore*, see Cropper, *The Ideal of Painting*, 146. Noteworthy, too, is the portrait of Poussin printed at the beginning of Bellori's *Vita*, in which the figure holds a portfolio bearing the inscription "DE. LUM. ET. UMB." This portrait is a fusion of the self-portraits in Paris and East Berlin.

[18] See Anthony Blunt, "Poussin's Notes on Painting," *Journal of the Warburg and Courtauld Institutes* 1 (1937–1938), 344–51.

[19] Bellori, *Le vite*, 481 and Anthony Blunt, ed., *Nicholas Poussin: Lettres et propos sur l'art* (Paris, 1964), 174. See also Blunt, "Poussin's Notes on Painting," 347, who writes that the passage quoted "implies scorn for the sensuous charm of colors."

[20] Charles Jouanny, ed., *Correspondance de Nicolas Poussin* (Paris, 1911), 461–4.

Colors, in short, are for Poussin crucial to the creation of "la forme et la ressemblance de la chose vue." The importance of color for the creation of a lifelike image is just what Venetian artists of the Renaissance had proved, and we clearly see here Poussin's affinity to his illustrious predecessors.

In another of his "observations," one that echoes phrases from Leon Battista Alberti's treatise of painting (*De Pictura*) Poussin writes of the limits or "termini" of drawing and color: "the painting will be elegant when the greatest limits are joined to the first by way of the middle in such a way that they do not converge too weakly or with harshness of lines and colors, and here we may speak of the friendliness or adversity of colors and their limits."[21] Alberti explains that there is a "certa amicizia," a certain friendship, among colors and recommends the placing of one color against another, different one, such as red next to green, and light colors against dark ones. Poussin is not entirely clear about the meaning he attached to the word "termini," but judging from the context of Alberti's thought and from the artist's reference in another of his "observations" to the "gentle harmony of the lights next to the darks" in paintings, we may interpret him to be referring to the subtle or friendly joining of the tones and values of colors.[22] Colors must be joined one to another in an harmonious and friendly fashion. And a frame gilded with dull gold preserves the harmonious relations among the tones and values of colors by blending gently with them.

The prominence given to the frames in Poussin's *Self-Portrait* (plate 31) would suggest that he might well have wanted to remind Chantelou of the importance of protecting the subtle harmony of colors with frames gilded with a dull gold, just as he had explained in his letter of 1639 about his *Israelites Gathering Manna*, mentioned earlier. But, even if Poussin did not intend such an allusion, there is some evidence to suggest that his patron very well understood his desire for a particular kind of frame for his paintings and, hence, may have "read" the frames in the *Self-Portrait* as signs of that desire.

An entry in Chantelou's well-known journal recording Gianlorenzo Bernini's visit to France in 1665, fifteen years after Poussin

---

[21] Bellori, *Le vite*, 479; and Leon Battista Alberti, *De Pictura*, ed. Cecil Grayson (Bari, 1975), 86.

[22] Bellori, *Le vite*, 479.

delivered the Louvre *Self-Portrait*, tells of a conversation with the sculptor about the importance of borders in tapestries.[23] Chantelou's famous guest held that such works should have simple borders because much splendor and variety are not necessary in them and cited Raphael's designs for the Vatican tapestries as examples of good border-design. Rather, the borders should serve only as a limit to the scene represented. Bernini continued that the same is true for paintings, which need frames that produce the least confusion and the greatest clarity; that is to say, simple rather than ornate borders.

Chantelou responded that Poussin, who, he said, would have agreed with the Cavaliere, was always recommending such simple frames without burnished gold. In courteous regard for the occupation of Bernini, Chantelou, recalling Vasari, goes on to underscore what he has just said by very appropriately remarking that Michelangelo did not like ornate niches and held that the sculpture was the only ornament of the niche.

The point of Chantelou's conversation with Bernini is that a work of art, whether it be a tapestry, a painting, or a sculpture, will always need a simple, unobtrusive terminus, one that will not distract the viewer's attention from the work itself but will separate it from its surroundings, "satisfying a need for clarity in isolating the image for the eye."[24] Poussin, in his letter of 1639 to Chantelou, defines a similar function for frames, but he does not mention that the frames of his paintings should be simple in design. Perhaps, then, Chantelou, while conversing with Bernini, recalled Poussin's *Self-Portrait*, in which the frames are quite simply designed. In all probability, however, Chantelou understood Poussin's reasons for wanting simple frames gilded with matte gold for his paintings, frames that, in Bernini's terms, produce the least confusion and the greatest clarity, but the problem of preserving the harmony of colors did not arise in the conversation.

For Bellori, Poussin's *Self-Portrait* was above all an expression of the artist's noble character and appearance, but also a kind of

[23] Paul Fréart de Chantelou [ed. L. Lalanne], "Journal de voyage du Cavalier Bernin in France," *Gazette des Beaux-Arts* 2nd ser., 23 (1881): 276.

[24] Quoting Meyer Schapiro, "On Some Problems in the Semiotics of Visual Art: Field and Vehicle in Image-Signs," *Semiotica* 1 (1969): 228. Schapiro's understanding of the function of frames is remarkably similar to that of Bernini and Poussin.

monument to the love of the art of painting on the part of Chantelou, who, in turn, admired the painter's nobility. No doubt the
patron understood the painting in much the same way, and the figure of painting, as Posner suggests, may have caused him to recall
as well Poussin's thoughts on art, his intellect, and his awareness of
the intellectual difficulty of painting. In addition, the canvases may
have exemplified for him a practical side of Poussin's nature, his
desire to have his works appropriately framed, and his concern for
the preservation of the harmony of his colors, which he thought
properly prepared frames ensured.

Poussin's concern for the colors in his paintings also denotes
the continued debt the artist owed to the Venetian tradition. Early
in his career he had pursued a painterly manner, and near the end
of his life, he returned to that manner. In the interim, he expresses
a desire for a particular kind of frame, one that would preserve the
harmony of his colors, a harmony that he had observed in the
works of his illustrious Venetian predecessors.

10: Father and Son

THE PEACE OF PASSAROWITZ in 1718, following war with the Turks, marks the end of La Serenissima, as the Venetian republic was often called, as a major political and military power. As if in tacit recognition of this unpleasant fact, the inhabitants of the city began to enjoy themselves with hitherto uncharacteristic abandon. Not only did they seek their own pleasure, they invited the rest of Europe to join their almost perpetual Carnival. They "set up shop as merchants of delight and the foreigners, more numerous than before, came flocking as though to an assignation, drawn spellbound to the promising, marvelous city where pleasure was an article of faith and poetry the law of common day."[1] It is just this enchanting mixture of pleasure and poetry that yet attracts us to eighteenth-century Venice and rewards our study of it at every turn.

If the century saw the political decline of the city — the social and moral decline seem to be a post-Revolution myth — it also saw a remarkable renascence of artistic and intellectual life, for after the brilliant period of Titian, Tintoretto, Veronese, Aretino and Monteverdi in the sixteenth century, the arts in Venice had declined during the next century. We need only mention the names of the liberal reformer of theater, Carlo Goldoni, and the conservative champion of the *commedia dell'arte*, Carlo Gozzi, to evoke the vital controversy then surrounding the Venetian theater. In music, the city could boast of a number of outstanding performers and composers, among them Giacomo Albinoni, Bernardo Galuppi and, best of all, Antonio Vivaldi. In painting, we encounter an entire galaxy of talented artists, among whom are Antonio Canaletto, Francesco Guardi, Sebastiano Ricci, Giambattista Piazzetta, and two Tiepolos, Giambattista (1696–1770) and Giandomenico (1727–1804).

Giambattista Tiepolo is widely recognized as one of the greatest painters of the eighteenth century and the last major figure among the many distinguished artists who worked in the tradition of Italian art beginning with Giotto. Like many of his Venetian predeces-

---

[1] Maurice Andrieux, *Daily Life in Venice in the Time of Casanova*, trans. Mary Fritton (New York and Washington, 1972), 105.

sors (for example, the Vivarini and the Bellini), he was the head of a family of painters and employed two sons as assistants, Lorenzo (1736–1776) and Giandomenico. Whereas Lorenzo seems never to have become an independent artist, Domenico achieved autonomy, and recent studies have made progress in describing the distinctive character of his work.[2] He is now, after a long period of relative obscurity, praised especially for his graphic works. Still, because of the close association of father and son, it is often difficult to distinguish their hands with absolute certainty.

A case in point is a painting that may have been part of a series of six representing scenes from the Passion of Christ, namely, the *Crucifixion of Christ* in the Saint Louis Art Museum (plate 34), which various scholars have attributed to either one or the other of the two artists. Both attributions have merit, but recently George Knox has most convincingly argued that the painting should be viewed as a collaborative work.[3] Here, however, for the sake of convenience we shall refer to the picture as a work by Giambattista.

In this easel-size canvas, we see the crucifixion of Christ and the two thieves. Behind them, above a range of mountains, darkness falls over the land, as is set forth in Biblical accounts of the event. Christ, His eyes open, gazes downward at His mother, wrapped in a sky-blue mantle and supported from behind by a woman, perhaps Mary, wife of Cleophas and the Virgin's sister. There are also on this side of the picture various other figures, including a large oriental man, seated on the ground and wearing a red cloak and a red and white turban, who looks in the direction of the grief-stricken women. Beside him lies a drum, which may have been used to tap out some sort of death march in accompaniment to the procession up Golgotha, and a single log, a relic, perhaps, of a previous scene of cruelty and torture. Just to the right of the center of the painting is a man on horseback, identifiable as Saint Longinus. He, according to legend, is the Roman soldier who was converted to belief in Christ on this occasion. Behind the crosses is a crowd of people, among whom, in the lower right-hand corner, are Nicodemus and Joseph of Arimathea bringing the ladder with which they will take

[2] See, for example, Michael Levey, *Giambattista Tiepolo: His Life and Art* (New Haven and London, 1986), 133–41.

[3] George Knox, *Giambattista and Domenico Tiepolo: A Catalogue Raisonné of the Chalk Drawings* 2 vols. (Oxford, 1980), 1: 299 cat. no. P. 69. Knox provides further bibliography.

His body down from the Cross. Above them, standing on an out-cropping of rock, are two figures who observe the scene from a distance as they are slowly engulfed in the mist of the darkening clouds. On the other side of the painting, two birds, silhouetted against the bright, blue sky, soar freely on the wind.

Surprisingly, the *Crucifixion*, as a work of art in the fullest sense, has not received a great deal of discussion from critics and art historians, perhaps, at least in part, because it presents no problems requiring solution, except the question of attribution. The iconography, although complex, is unambiguous; indeed, it is perfectly understandable to anyone who has knowledge of the story. Still, this is a stupendous work of art and therefore deserving of appreciation and intense viewing.

The author of an article in the *Nuova Veneta Gazzetta* of March 20, 1762 reports that he had overheard Giambattista Tiepolo say that if the painter's works are to appeal to rich, noble people, who buy pictures of great value, then the artist must aspire "to the sublime, to the heroic and to perfection."[4] Certainly, in the *Crucifixion* (plate 34), Giambattista aspired to and obtained just those qualities. This scene of high pathos, reflecting the passionate, yet elevated mind of the artist, achieves a certain perfection in its *grandezza* and loftiness, qualities which set it apart from the mundane reality that occupied some of his contemporaries, such as Canaletto and Pietro Longhi. There is also in this painting evidence of a particular aspect of the artist's singular *virtù*, his fondness for the exotic and fanciful. This fondness is manifested specifically in the oriental, Turkish looking men who make up most of the crowd. In their strange hats and rich robes, they are like magicians from a distant land, the mysterious East, where the Crucifixion took place.

The same kind of men people many of Giambattista's (and Giandomenico's) works, including those drawings and prints identified as *capricci* and *scherzi di fantasia*, which titles, borrowed from music, indicate "a fantastic or extravagant artistic inspiration and gener-

---

[4] The text is cited by Francis Haskell, *Patrons and Painters: A Study in the Relations Between Italian Art and Society in the Age of the Baroque* (New Haven and London, 1980), 253 note 2: "Ho udito dire dal Signor Tiepolo stesso...che li Pittore devono procurare di riuscire nelle opere grandi, cioè in quelle che possano piacere alli Signori Nobili, e ricchi, perchè questi fanno la fortuna de' Professori, e non già l'altra gente, la quale non può comparare Quadri di molto valore. Quindi è che la mente del Pittore deve sempre tendere al Sublime, all'Eroico, alla Perfezione."

ally refer to compositions without an easily recognizable subject, resulting from a whim of the imagination."[5] Although the subject matter of the *Crucifixion* is easily recognizable, the oriental looking figures retain something of the whimsical and capricious found in Tiepolo's drawings and prints. They are also examples of what the artist's contemporaries referred to as *caricature* or exaggerations.

When Giandomenico's series of paintings representing the Stations of the Cross was unveiled in Venice, it was criticized in a letter of 1749 by Pietro Visconti, a Milanese painter of *quadratura* who later worked with Giambattista in the Villa Pisano at Strà.

> The work has not met with much [acclaim], although it has been entirely retouched by his father's hand and various parts were made after his designs. In regard to the reputation of the son, even the invention of the paintings are criticized, for in them he has made all of the figures dressed in costumes of foreign countries — some Spanish, some Slavs and others caricatures — so that they say that in those days that sort of person was not found but that he made them [in that way] because they are better suited to his character.[6]

Though the author goes on begrudgingly to acknowledge the general appreciation of the Tiepolos's "novità" or novelty, his letter, while criticizing Giandomenico's art, is also a thinly veiled attack on Giambattista. According to Visconti, whose taste tended toward the classical, Giandomenico's inventions, in part the productions of his father, are too fanciful, with the result that his paintings lack historical accuracy. Here we see the age-old conflict between the expectations of literal minded souls and the demands of those beings for whom imagination takes precedent.

---

5 Adriano Mariuz, "The Drawings of Giambattista Tiepolo," in *Masterpieces of Eighteenth-Century Venetian Drawing*, trans. David Smith (New York, 1983), 25.

6 Eduoardo Arslan, "Quattro lettere di Pietro Visconti a Gian Pietro Ligari," *Rivista archeologica dell'antica provincia e diocesi di Como* 133 (1952): 69–70: "...l'opera non à incontrato molto benche sia ripasata tutta per mane di suo Padre e diversi pezi fatti di pianta sui benchè sino il nome del figlio come pur linvenzione de Pitori è gritichata per eserli li chostumi à fatti tutte figure straniere parte vistiti all spagnola, schiavoni e altre carichature che dichono che in quel tempo non si ritrovata tal sorte di gente ma che lui li à fatti perchè meglio comodono al suo caratro."

The *Crucifixion*, then, exemplifies one aspect of Giambattista's *virtù*, his fondness for the extravagant and capricious; it also demonstrates another, quite different facet of his imagination. At first the horse on the right seems to present nothing unusual to the viewer, but long contemplation reveals that it is literally too small in relation to the rest of the composition, too small even in relation to its rider. Perhaps Giambattista was used to seeing relatively small horses, but a more probable case is that he has slightly adjusted the size of the animal to the content of the picture. In other words, the horse's energetic movement is closely related to the near frenzied activity of the crowd and had Giambattista made the animal any larger or any smaller that activity would have been either diminished on the one hand, or overwhelmed on the other.

If the *Crucifixion* throws certain aspects of Giambattista's *virtù* and of his mastery of the art of painting into relief, it also reveals his debt to the long and deep tradition in which he worked. The loose, seemingly rapid application of the paint, for example, is unthinkable without Titian's late works or the paintings of Tintoretto and Veronese. Like that of those masters, his brushwork, though applied more broadly, is both descriptive and expressive. That is to say, his relatively long, gracefully applied strokes describe the forms of his composition and at the same time enhance the expression of the painting as a whole. Indeed, the movement of the brushwork in the lower portion of the painting is played against the relatively flat area of the dark cloud so as to underscore one of the painting's fundamental contrasts, that between the tumultuous activity of the crowd and horse and the calm and solemn figures of Christ, His mother and followers.

On the other hand, Tiepolo's brushwork differs from that of his Renaissance predecessors insofar as he employs an innovative combination of *disegno* and *colore*. In the sixteenth century, these two parts of painting were understood by virtually all art theorists as distinct steps in the act of creation. *Disegno* or drawing was the underlying linear composition and *colore* or *colorito* the application of paint to the drawing in order to give it a lifelike appearance. By the seventeenth century *disegno* had come also to imply certain qualities — discipline, restraint, balance, control and idealized forms — such as we find in Poussin's mature paintings, whereas *colore* suggested spontaneity, variety, asymmetry, texture, and a direct response to nature.[7] Though Tiepolo clearly works in the tradition of *colore*, his manner is a fusion of drawing and coloring in a particular sense, for he combines relatively broad areas of textured color and dark lines of various thicknesses, both of which are applied loosely to the canvas.

This combination, in which *disegno* acquires the spontaneity of the painterly, is visible only when a painting like the *Crucifixion* is viewed from a relatively short distance. As one moves back, away from the painting, the lines seem to disappear but their function becomes apparent. They are used to clarify forms, to give them a precision they would otherwise lack. They also blend harmoniously into the overall pattern of chiaroscuro, adding emphasis to that pattern. For example, the dark, broken lines of the oriental's red cloak not only help to define its folds, they also merge into the general pattern of light and shadow, and thereby enhance the painting's naturalistic illusion.

In regard to color, there is another, perhaps even more significant difference between the manner of Tiepolo and that of his predecessors. As John Addington Symonds explained almost a century ago, Giambattista is the master of *plein air* effects, which he achieved not in the out-of-doors but in his studio "where a hitherto conventional scheme of light and colour held undisputed sway." Tiepolo, as Symonds also explains, derived these effects from Venice itself.

> His key of colour, wonderfully clear and luminous, is settled by the harmonies between weather-mellowed marble, light blue sky, russet or ochre-tinted sails, vivid vegetable greens, sunburnt faces, and patches of bright hues in the costumes of sailors and the common people, all subdued and softened by the pearly haze "of moisture bred," which bathes Venetian landscape in the warmth of early summer.[8]

Symonds is speaking here of Giambattista's color and light in general, but his description is applicable, with only slight variation, to

---

[7] For a brief but accurate discussion of this topic as it pertains to seventeenth-century art, see Harris, *Andrea Sacchi*, 43 note 17.

[8] John Addington Symonds,"On an Altar-piece by Tiepolo," in *In the Key of Blue and Other Prose Essays* (New York and London, 1918) [1st edition, 1893], 45–6.

the *Crucifixion*.

On the right-hand side of the painting, the subdued dark cloud, covering roughly two-thirds of the sky, is an almost flat, leaden gray. On the left this gray, which now becomes more varied in tone and value, rises to a light blue sky. Between these two areas is an S-shaped mass of pinkish, flesh-colored clouds. At the horizon a range of gray mountains, reminiscent of the Eugenean hills, is punctuated by a single peak lying brilliantly white in the sunlight. Some of the colors of the sky are echoed in the lower portion of the painting, for example, in the grayish white of the body of Christ and the horse below Him. But this lower portion of the painting is composed mostly of earth-colors — vegetable greens, neutral ochres, russets and dark browns — relieved by patches of bright color arranged around the center of the canvas. The blood-red of the oriental's cloak and the cloth held by the man behind him is in harmony with the bright red of the Virgin's tunic and of the dress of the woman behind her, and these in turn are balanced by the luminous orange-red of the banner behind Christ. There is also a brilliant touch of red in the tassel decorating the lance, in the center of the painting, with which Christ's side is about to be pierced. The clear, bright blue of the Virgin's mantle is a purer form of the lighter blue of the sky and is echoed by touches of the same color in the crowd and the soldier on horseback. This harmonious arrangement of bright and neutral colors is united by the silvery sheen cast upon it by the strong light flooding the scene from the left.

Giambattista's debt to the Venetian Renaissance tradition extends beyond brushwork and coloring. Like many Venetian painters of his time, he owed much to the art of Paolo Veronese. In the instance of the *Crucifixion*, the composition is ultimately derived from a painting like Veronese's picture of the same subject in the Louvre (plate 35). Here the crosses are grouped to the left of the painting, while the other side is filled with a darkening sky and a view of Jerusalem in the distance. Tiepolo's placement of the crosses is also off-center, but not as radically as that in Veronese's work. Moreover, Giambattista's composition is much more complex. The soldier's lance, the ladder, the log in the lower left-hand corner, and the seated oriental — these elements are arranged as a series of strong diagonals played against the equally strong verticals of the crosses, and this counter-rhythm lends his picture a sense of spatial volume within which there occurs a lively and dramatic movement. By contrast, the space around Veronese's figures appears to be relatively shallow and his composition relatively static.

Against the compositional structure comprising verticals and diagonals, Tiepolo employs another structure comprising graceful
S-shaped lines. For instance, the downward-moving curve of the
body of Christ echoes that of the thief on His right-hand side. This
downward movement suggests the weight of the two figures' bodies as they hang on their respective crosses, and in the case of the
thief, this sense of gravity's effect is enhanced by the upward movement of the undulating curve formed by the weightless clouds
behind him and by the gentle, arching bend of the Virgin's pose.

Not only is Giambattista's *Crucifixion* indebted to the example
of sixteenth-century Venetian painting, it is also draws upon the
Renaissance tradition of art in general. One important instance of
this is the way in which several of the figures have their faces turned away from the viewer, most notably the seated oriental and the
soldier on the horse. This kind of figure has its origin in such
works as Giotto's *Lamentation Over the Dead Body of Christ* in the
Arena Chapel, Padua (plate 36), in which two women in the lower
left-hand portion of the scene are viewed from behind. Inspite of
the four centuries separating the two paintings, Tiepolo's figures
function in a way similar to that in which Giotto's women do, a
function that was explained in the fifteenth century by Leon Battista Alberti in his treatise on painting.

Alberti discusses a picture by Timanthes in which, he says, the
Ancient artist wanted to show the grief of Menelaus at the sacrifice
of his daughter, Iphigenia. Timanthes, Alberti continues, could not
find a suitable a way to represent an expression of grief on the face
of the distraught father, and so depicted him with his head wrapped in a cloth; by such means the artist left it to the viewers to
imagine that which they could not actually see ("non avendo in
che modo mostrare la tristezza del padre, a lui avolse uno panno al
capo, e così lassò si pensasse qual non si vedea suo acerbissimo mer-
ore").[9] Similarly, in Giotto's painting, because the viewer cannot
see the faces of the two women with their backs turned, he must
imagine their grief as they sit in contemplate of the lifeless body of
Christ. Likewise, Tiepolo's oriental man and the soldier on horseback engage the viewer's imagination; the beholder is called upon
to imagine their expressions.

Tiepolo's figures, again like Giotto's, serve another purpose, too.

[9] Alberti, *De Pictura*, para. 42. Alberti is here recalling Quintilian.

Because their backs are turned towards the picture plane, they enhance the viewers' feeling of being present at this Crucifixion — their sense that they are part of the crowd witnessing the event. The beholders, in other words, imaginatively stand in a position analogous to the figures in the painting, who are grouped on the other side of the crosses, which group also heightens the viewers' feeling of being present here. We are made part of the crowd gathered at Golgotha on this momentous occasion, and, by implication, we are invited to meditate upon and imaginatively to participate in the scene before us.

At first glance the viewer is enthralled, or stupefied, by the lifelike action of the scene, which seems to represent a particular moment in time. In this moment, Christ looks down from the Cross at His mother and her companions, while the tumultuous crowd surges around Him and the soldier's horse lunges forward with sheer animal power. After this initial impression, however, the viewer begins to see that the painting actually represents a series of separate moments in the Passion narrative and contains elements that allude to other incidents in that story. Like Rembrandt in his *Hundred Guilder Print*, Tiepolo gathers together and unites various moments, and allusions to moments into a kind of mosaic that seemingly represents a single, eternal instant.[10]

The Last Supper, we recall as we stand here on Golgotha, has been eaten and drunk. Barabbas has been released, and Jesus has been mocked. Simon of Cyrene, the Cross-bearer, is lost in the crowd. Christ has told the daughters of Jerusalem to weep not for Him but for themselves, for the time of the green tree is past and the days of the dry tree are near, when the barren will be called blessed, and the people will implore the mountains to fall upon them. Significantly, the Cross is colored green, for it is resurrected, miraculously taking root and spreading its branches far and wide.

When He arrived here, they gave Him a bitter drink to ease His impending pain — vinegar mixed with gall, or wine mixed with myrrh — but though He was thirsty, He did not drink. Then, at the third hour, they nailed Him and the two thieves to the crosses. While that was going on, He said, "Father, forgive them; for they know not what they do." About this time, too, Pilate wrote out the titulus (I. N. R. I), proclaiming Him "King of the Jews" and had it

[10] For Rembrandt's influence on the Tiepolos, see F. W. Robinson, "Rembrandt's Influence in Eighteenth-Century Venice," *Nederlands Kunsthistorisch Jaarboek* 18 (1967): 167–96.

placed at the very top of His Cross.

Meanwhile, the soldiers on duty, having set the crosses upright, divided up His garments and cast lots for His coat, which was woven, they say, without a seam. Perhaps the young man to the left with his face turned away from the viewer has won His coat, for he stands emotionally isolated, as he holds a blood-red cloth.

As the crowd filed past the crosses, wagging their heads, they mocked and reviled Him, saying "Save thyself, come down from the Cross," and "Let the King of Israel come down that we might see and believe." One of the thieves, casting the same in His teeth, said, "If you are the Christ, save yourself and us," but the other said to him, "Do you not fear God, seeing that you are crucified with Him? We receive just punishment, but He has done nothing wrong." And turning to Christ, this thief said, "Remember me when you come into your kingdom," and He answered him saying, "Verily I say unto thee, today shalt thou be with me in paradise." This is one of the moments of Tiepolo's painting, for the mouth of the thief to His right is open as if he speaks to Christ, while the other thief silently writhes in pain. Indeed, Tiepolo masterfully portrays this complex relationship between Christ and the two thieves.

The downward curve of the body of the good thief echoes that of the body of Christ, and the position of his arms and hands in relation to his cross is like that of Christ. By these means and by his position to the right of Christ, the repentant thief is identified as such. Although he is not illuminated by the light shining from the left-hand side of the painting, we see his body and facial expression.

The unrepentant thief is crucified in a manner different from that in which his companions are. His legs are bound with a rope high up on his cross, and his left arm is thrown up and over its top. Moreover, unlike Christ and the other thief, he is both physically and emotionally animated by the pain and horror of crucifixion. Surprisinglyly, the intense, pearly light illuminating Christ also shines on the body of this unrepentant man, as if to suggest that even though he has rejected the Logos, he too will inherit the benefits of the Green Tree, which are His triumph over death and sin.

Since the sixth hour, the shadows have begun to lengthen, and the sky has begun to grow dark. Now it is the ninth hour. His mother, almost overcome with grief, stands at the foot of the Cross. Behind and just to the right of her kneels that consummate sinner, the prostitute Mary Magdalene, wrapped in a white garment, sign of her purity in Christ, and holding her hand to her chest as she gazes upward into the true Light. She, we recall, once washed Christ's feet, the same feet that are now immediately in front of her, and she will be the one who first sees Him after the Resurrection, though she will momentarily mistake Him for a gardener tending the world of the New Eden, a world redeemed of sin. The bearded man behind the Magdalene, lost in lust after her physical beauty, knows none of this. He bends his head close to her, so that only she will hear his lecherous whispers, so close, indeed, that she can feel his hot, damp breath upon her neck.

On the other side of the Virgin, her sister Mary, wife of Cleophas, supports her and looks down at one of the disciples, the beloved John. Just a few minutes ago Christ cried out to the Virgin, "Woman, behold thy son!" and to John, "Behold thy mother!" that he might take her into his own house. Mary is still unsteady from the sight of her Son, and John, transfixed by His words, remains kneeling before the Cross with his hands held in prayerful reverence, while a man from the crowd, holding what appears to be a legionary standard, symbol of temporal power and authority, listens intrusively. Mere courtesy has no place here.

Then He cried out in a loud voice words that echo still through the painting, "Eloi, Eloi, lama sabachthami" ("Lord! Lord! Why hast thou forsaken me?"). The people misunderstood his words, thinking that He had called upon Elias, and they waited to see if the prophet would come to help Him. He asked for drink, and a sponge dipped in vinegar was lifted on a hyssop to His lips. Finally, yielding up the ghost, He said, "Father, unto thy hands I commend my spirit," and then "It is finished." With those words the veil of the temple was rent in twain from top to bottom, the earth began to tremble, the graves of the saints were opened and the rocks were split apart. Seeing these things, that brute of a centurion, Longinus, cried out, as if in recognition of a great truth long ignored, "Truly He was the Son of God!"

Later, that the bodies might not remain hanging on the Sabbath, the soldiers came to break the legs of the crucified, but finding Him already dead, they only pierced His side. These, too, are moments in Tiepolo's scene, for at its center an anonymous hand, holding a tasseled lance, rises above the crowd towards His body, and Longinus reels at his awakening, almost tumbling from his horse, which lunges forward in the excitement.

Presently, the sun will begin to set, and soon will be the Sabbath. Joseph of Arimathaea, wise and just counsellor, who also waits for the Kingdom, will go to Pilate asking for the Body. He and good Nicodemus will approach the Cross, just as we see them here, to take Him down. They will anoint His lifeless body with a mixture of myrrh and aloes and will wrap it in clean linen and place it in a tomb carved out of living rock.

At last our attention is drawn to the heavens, which, with its contrast of light and dark, looks very much like the sky over Venice in one of its most dramatic moods. And this natural drama is perfectly suited to the action of the narrative below, in which the Light of the World dies, only to be resurrected. The dark, somber, almost flat gray clouds rolling in from the right threaten to fill up the spacious, light-filled sky on the left, where two birds, like two souls suddenly released from the confines of earthly existence, drift and soar on the wind with complete freedom.

Giambattista Tiepolo is most often admired for his fresco decorations, those vast walls and ceilings which only he could turn into brilliant spaces of vital luminosity. His son, Domenico, also a decorator is best known for his drawings, particularly the series known as *Divertimenti per le ragazzi*. Less often admired are the Tiepolos's religious works on canvas, of which there are many.[11] Perhaps, as in the case of Veronese, this is because decoration and religious emotion are viewed as incompatible, or perhaps it is because in the eighteenth century religion, especially Christianity, had already begun to lose its place at the center of human life. Whatever the reason for this dearth of admiration, the *Crucifixion*, whether painted by father, by son, or by both in collaboration, is proof of the depth of religious conviction and feeling of which the Tiepolos were capable — proof that is, as Hetzer explains, of their ability to combine creative imagination and religious conception "to form a living whole," even in the age when "enlightenment" was too often viewed with unrestrained optimism.[12] The *Crucifixion* is proof, too, of their ability to crystallize their convictions and emotions in works of exquisite beauty.

[11] A welcome exception to this state of affairs is the recently published study by William L. Barcham, *The Religious Paintings of Giambattista Tiepolo: Piety and Tradition in Eighteenth-Century Venice* (Oxford, 1989).

[12] Theodor Hetzer, "Francisco Goya and the Crisis of Art around 1800," in *Goya in Perspective*, ed. Fred Licht (Englewood Cliffs, 1966), 96.

Envoi

THE ESSENTIAL CHARACTER, as well as the history, of Venetian art are often viewed in terms of coloring or *colorito*, a view that has its origin in Vasari, who held that such artists as Giorgione and Titian, among others, were outstanding in this particular aspect of painting but deficient in design or drawing. Vasari also held that the Venetian painter's regard for sensuous impressions is in distinct contrast to the Central Italian regard for the more intellectual aspect of art, *disegno*. This understanding of the art of Venice has remained popular even unto our own day, but in the nineteenth century, Venetian coloring was also seen to be in the service of a larger goal.

> To idealize the sensualities of the universe; to achieve for colour what the Florentines had done for form; to invest the external splendours of human life at one of its most gorgeous epochs with the dignity of the highest art; to vindicate the long forgotten title of the body to respect; to prove the sanity and majesty of the flesh, was what these giant spirits lived to do.[13]

No one would deny that the celebration of physical existence and the naturalistic portrayal of the colors of nature in all of their sensuous fullness are hallmarks of Venetian painting from the works of Giovanni Bellini in the fifteenth century to those of the Tiepolo in the eighteenth. These ways of characterizing the art of the Lagoon, however, have had certain unfortunate consequences.

For instance, if we understand Venetian painting only in terms of its coloring, our history of it will tend to separate too emphatically its earlier and later phases. Because Venetian artists from the Renaissance onward tended to idealize sensuous impressions so

---

[13] John Addington Symonds, "Venetian Painting," *Westminster Review* 196 (April 1873):183–4.

gorgeously, many have come to believe that this was their primary, if not there only concern. On the whole, we have too often ignored the fact that subject matter and its disposition were also of importance for them, just as they were for Florentine and Roman artists. More precisely, Venetian painters in general viewed subject matter as an opportunity for the exercise of their *fantasia*, for the creation of images that convey novel meanings, whether those images be religious or otherwise. Pre-Renaissance art, then, is united to the work of its heirs in its penchant for the imaginative handling of subject matter.

Moreover, if we identify the sensuous element in Venetian art only with coloring, we shall overlook at least one important similarity among the works of, say, Giambono, Titian and the Tiepolos. Giambono, like other late-Gothic painters, liberally used raised and gilded gesso on his panels. In works like his *Saint Michael Archangel* (plate 2), for example, the figure's crown, portions of his dalmatic, and the monstrance atop the sphere in his right hand all project away from the picture's surface, making it, in effect, a combination of painting and relief-sculpture. As has been often remarked, a tactile dimension is also present in Titian's late works especially. In those works not only the paint itself but also the weave of the canvas are central to the impact of the painting as such. The same is true of oil paintings by the Tiepolos, in which impasto is almost always a significant feature of the form. The art of the fourteenth and early fifteenth centuries, then, is linked to Renaissance and eighteenth-century art not only in its inventiveness but also inasmuch as both possess a tactile dimension, which dimension, however, is manifested differently in each period.

Typical elements of Venetian painting, as the foregoing essays have sought to establish, are its inventive approach to subject matter and its sensuousness, both in its regard for the colors of nature and its appeal to the tactile sense. These two qualities, in turn, are integrally related to the poetic appeal of Venetian art, to its awareness of the unconscious and irrational, and to its vision of the fusion of flesh and spirit. Moreover, this quality of poetic suggestiveness engages our own *fantasia*, working its magic upon us in ways that we often cannot explain, evoking poetic experiences in us and poetic responses to art. Sensuous, physical beauty; novelty and fantasy; and poetic suggestiveness — herein lie the deep enchantment of Venetian art and the eternal vitality of its artful panels and fabrics.

Appendix A

Veronese and the Tribunal of the Inquisition

The document recording Veronese's appearance before the Tribunal of the Inquisition was first published in a French translation by Armand Baschet, "Paul Véronèse au Tribunal du Saint Office, a Venise (1573)," *Gazette des Beaux-Arts* 1st ser., 23 (1867): 372–8. For this translation I have used the Italian text in Philipp Fehl, "Veronese and the Inquisition: A Study of the Subject-Matter of the so-called 'Feast in the House of Levi'," *Gazette des Beaux-Arts* 6th ser., 58 (1961): 349–52. My translation reflects some of Fehl's suggestions about the meaning of the text in various places and the course of the interrogation.

Sunday, 18 July 1573

Paolo Caliari Veronese, painter and inhabitant of the parish of San Samuele, having been called before the Holy Office of the Holy Tribunal of God and questioned about his name and surname, responds as above.

Asked about his profession, he [Veronese] responds, "I paint and make figures."
He [interrogator] says, "Do you know why you have been called here?"
He [Veronese] responds, "No, sir."
He says, "Can you imagine why?"
He responds, "I can well imagine."
He says, "Say that which you imagine."
He responds, "According to what I was told by the Reverend Fathers, that is to say, the Prior of Santi Giovanni e Paolo, whose name I do not know, who told me that he had been here and that Your Illustrious Lordships had given the order to have a Magdalene made in place of the dog [in the painting], and I answered him that I would willingly do that and anything else for my honor and that of my picture. [Missing question?] But that I did not feel that the figure of the Magdalene would serve just as

well [as the dog], [missing question?] for many reasons which I will give any time I am given an occasion on which I may speak of them."

He says, "Which picture is this of which you have spoken?"

He responds, "This is the picture of the Last Supper, which Jesus Christ took with his apostles [missing question?] in the house of Simon."

He says, "Where is this picture?"

He responds, "In the refectory of the friars of Santi Giovanni e Paolo."

He says, "Is it [painted] on a wall, on a panel, or on canvas?"

He responds, "On canvas."

He says, "How many feet high is it?"

He responds, "It could be seventeen feet [high]."

He says, "How wide is it?"

He responds, "About thirty-nine feet [wide]."

He says, "At this Supper of the Lord you have painted servants?"

He responds, "Yes, sir."

He says, "Tells us how many servants and the effect that each one of them makes."

He responds, "There is the master of the inn, Simon. Other than this [figure] — I made under this figure a steward, who, I pretended had come for his amusement to see how things were going at the table." Then he added that there are many figures [in the painting], "so that there is much that I put in the picture that I do not remember."

He says, "Have you painted Suppers other than this one?"

He responds, "I made one of it in Verona at the reverend monks of San Nazzaro, which is in their refectory. I made one in the refectory of the Reverend Fathers of San Giorgio in Venice."

He said, "This is not a Supper. You were asked about the Supper of the Lord."

He responds, "I made one of it in the refectory of the Servi in Venice and one in the refectory of San Sebastiano here in Venice. And I made one in Padua at the Fathers of the Maddalena. And I do not recall having made others."

He says, "In this Supper that you made for Santi Giovanni e Paolo, what is the significance of the depiction of him from whose nose blood flows?"

He responds, "I made it for a servant, who because of some accident the blood can be coming from his nose."

He says, "Of what significance are those soldiers dressed as Germans, each with a halberd in one hand?"

He responds, "It requires that I say here twenty words."

He says that he say them.

He responds, "We painters [deleted: "have the"] take the license that poets and jesters take, and I made those two halberdiers, one who drinks and the other who eats near a stairway, who were put there so that they could perform some office appearing to me appropriate, which is that the master of the house was grand and rich, according to what I have been told, and would have such servants."

He says, "The one dressed as a buffoon with a parrot on his fist, to what effect have you painted him in that canvas?"

He responds, "For ornament, as one does."

He says, "At the table of the Lord, who are there?"

He responds, "The twelve apostles."

[Deleted: He says, "Do you know that Saint Peter is the first to dismember the lamb?"]

He says, "What effect does Saint Peter, who is the first [to dismember the lamb], make?"

He responds, "He quarters the lamb in order to give it to the other head of the table."

He says, "What effect does the other make?"

He responds, "He has a plate to receive that which Saint Peter gives to him."

He says, "What effect does the other make, who is near this one?"

He responds, "He is one who has a peg [i.e., toothpick] with which he cares for his teeth."

He says, "Whom do you truly believe one would have found at that Supper?"

He responds, "I believe that one would have found Christ and His apostles; but in the picture if some space presents itself, I adorn it with figures [deleted: "as I was commissioned and"] according to the invention."

He says, "Is there some person who commissioned you to paint in that picture Germans, buffoons and similar things?"

He responds, "No, sir; but the commission was to ornament the picture according to my own lights, which [painting] is large and has the capacity to hold many figures, as it seemed to me."

He says, "Are the ornaments which you painters usually make in your paintings or pictures customarily made appropriate and proportionate to the subject matter and the principal figures, or truly what is pleasing according to what comes to your imagination ["fantasia"] without any discretion or judgment?"

He responds, "I make paintings with consideration about that which is appropriate, as my intellect is capable."

Asked if it appears appropriate that at the Last Supper of the Lord he paints together buffoons, drunkards, Germans, dwarfs and other scurrilous things, he responds, "No, sir."

Asked, "Why, then, have you painted them?"

[He responds,] "I made them because I presupposed that they were outside the place where the Supper is taking place."

Asked, "Do you not know that in Germany and other places infested with heresy they are beginning with diverse paintings full of scurrility and similar inventions to mock and vituperate and make ridiculous the things of the Holy Catholic Church in order to teach false doctrine to stupid and ignorant people?"

He responds, "Sir, yes, that is bad: but I turn again to that which I said, that I am obliged to follow that which my superiors have done."

He says, "What have your superiors done? Have they perhaps done something similar?"

He responds, "Michelangelo in Rome, inside the pontifical chapel has painted our Lord Jesus Christ, His mother and Saint John, Saint Peter and the celestial court, all of which are shown in the nude, from the Virgin Mary on, in various acts with little reverence."

He says, "Do you not know that in painting the Last Judgment, in which one does not presume clothing or similar things, it is not necessary to paint clothing? And in those figures there is nothing that is not of the spirit; there are no buffoons, no dogs, no weapons, nor similar buffoonery. And does it appear because of this [painting in the Sistine Chapel] or because of some other example that you have done well in painting this picture in the manner in which it is, and do you wish to defend the picture [by saying] that it is good and decent?"

He responds, "Illustrious Lord, it is not that I wish to defend it; but I thought that I was doing well. And I did not consider so many things and was not thinking of causing confusion for anyone, all the more as those figures of buffoons are outside the place where Our Lord is."

After these things had been said, the judges decreed that the above-said Paolo should be obliged to correct and amend his picture, according to the decision of the Holy Tribunal, within a period of three months from the date of this reprimand, and all should be done at his expense and that if he did not amend the painting, he would be liable to penalties imposed by the Holy Tribunal. And thus, they decreed in the best manner possible.

Appendix B

Sixteenth- and Seventeenth-Century Descriptions
of Titian's *Martyrdom of Saint Peter Martyr*

1. Pietro Aretino

From Pietro Aretino, *Lettere sull'arte*, ed. Ettore Camesasca with commentary by Fidenzio Pertile. 3 vols. (Milan, 1957): 1:73.

Messer Sebastiano architettore, con piacere del molto diletto e del mediocre giudizio ch'io ho de la scultura, m'ha fatto vedere con le parole in che modo le pieghe facili ornano il panno de la Vergine che l'ingegno vostro mosso da la sua volontade lavora a mio nome. Hammi detto ancora come languidamente caschino le membra del Cristo che morto le avete posto in grembo con l'attitudine de l'arte; onde io ho veduto l'afflizione de la madre e la miseria del figliuolo prima ch'io l'abbia vista. Ma ecco nel raccontarmi egli il miracolo, che nasce da lo stile de la vostra industria, l'autore di quel San Pietro martire, che nel guardarlo converse e voi e Benvenuto ne l'imagine de lo stupore; e, fermati gli occhi del viso e le luci de l'intelletto in cotal opra, comprendeste tutti i vivi terrori de la morte e tutti i veri dolori de la vita ne la fronte e ne le carni del caduto in terra, maravigliandovi del freddo e del livido che gli appare ne la punta del naso e ne l'estremità del corpo, né potendo ritener la voce, lasciaste esclamarla, quando nel contemplar del compagno che fugge, gli scorgeste ne la sembianza il bianco de la viltà e il pallido de la paura. Veramente voi deste dritta sentenza al merito de la gran tavola nel dirmi che non era la più bella cosa in Italia. Che mirabil groppo di bambini è ne l'aria, che si dispicca dagli arbori, che la spargono dei tronchi e de le foglie loro; che paese raccolto ne la semplicità del suo naturale, che sassi erbosi bagna la acqua, che ivi fa corrente la vena uscita dal pennello del divin Tiziano!

2. Raffaello Borghini

From Raffaello Borghini, *Il Riposo*, 2 vols. (1584; reprint, Milan, 1967), 2:526.

...nella Chiesa di San Giovanni e Polo [è] la tavola dell'altare di San Pier Martire, dove é il detto Santo maggior del vivo entro à una boscaglia di alberi grandissima, caduto in terra, e ferito nella testa da un soldato, onde si conosce essere al punto della morte con altre figure, & in aria due Angeli nudi, che vengono da un lampo di cielo, che allumina il paese, e questa pittura è delle meglio intese, e con più diligenza condotte che mai facesse Titiano...

3. Lodovico Dolce

From Lodovico Dolce, *Dialogo della pittura, intitolato l'Aretino* [Venice, 1557] in *Trattati d'arte del cinquecento*, ed. Paola Barocchi, 3 vols. (Bari, 1960), 2:204.

In San Giovanni e Paolo fece la tavola del San Pietro Martire caduto in terra, con l'assassino che alza il braccio per ferirlo et un frate che fugge, con alcuni angioletti in aria che vengono giù come con la corona del martirio, et una macchia di paese con certi arbori di sambuco; le quali tutte cose sono da tanta perfezzione, che si possono più tosto invidiare che imitare. Mostra il frate di fuggire con un volto pieno di spavento, e par che si senta gridare, et il movimento è gagliardissimo, come di quello che aveva paura da dovero; senzaché il panno è fatto con una maniera che in altri non se ne vede esempio. La faccia del San Pietro contiene quella pallidezza che hanno i volti di coloro che si avicinano alla morte, e il santo sporge fuori un braccio et una mano di qualità che si può ben dire che la natura sia vinta dall'arte. Né mi estendo a narrarvi le bellezze della invenzione, del disegno e del colorito, perché elle sono a voi et a tutti note.

4. Giorgio Vasari

From Giorgio Vasari, *Le vite de' più eccellenti pittori, scultori ed architettori*, ed. Gaetano Milanesi, 9 vols. (Florence, 1906), 7:438–9.

Intanto, per tornare all'opere di Tiziano, egli fece la tavola all'altare di San Piero Martire nella chiesa di San Giovanni e Polo, facendovi maggior del vivo il detto santo martire dentro a una boscaglia d'alberi grandissimi, cascato in terra ed assalito dalla fierezza d'un soldato, che l'ha in modo ferito nella testa, che, essendo semivivo, se gli vede nel viso l'orrore della morte; mentre in un altro frate, che va innanzi fuggendo, si scorge lo spavento e timore della morte: in aria sono due angeli nudi, che vengono da un lampo di cielo, il quale dà lume al paese, che è bellissimo, ed a tutta l'opera insieme; la quale è la più compiuta, la più celebrata, e la maggiore e meglio intesa e condotta che altra, la quale in tutta sua vita Tiziano abbia fatto ancor mai.

5. Anonimo del Tizianello [Giovanni Maria Verdizotti?]

From Stefano Ticozzi, *Vite dei pittori vecelli di Cadore, libri quattro* (Milan, 1817), 68–9 note 1. Original text in [Anonimo del Tizianello,] *Breve compendio della vita del famoso Tiziano Vecelli, cavaliere et pittore, con l'arbore di sua vera consanguineità* (Venice, 1622).

In S. Giovanni e Paolo si vede S. Pietro M. che ferito, cadendo a terra, scopre il dolore e l'afflizione delle naturali passioni, ed il volto scolorato di chi da morte violenta viene percosso; e quel padre compagno di detto santo, ferito anch'egli, si vede tanto immerso nel dolore, e desideroso di salvarsi, che naturalmente si scopre il pallore nel volto, la natural difesa de' bracci e la fuga ne' piedi: oltre due angeli d'infinita bellezza, che discendono dal cielo, illuminando con apparente splendore l'oscurità dei figurati boschi.

6. Carlo Ridolfi

From Carlo Ridolfi, *Le maraviglie dell'arte*, ed. Detlev von Hadeln, 2 vols. (Rome, 1965), 2: 167–8.

Apparisce in questa il Santo, che nel ritorno al suo Convento di Como (dopò haver predicato con molta efficacia in Milano contra l'heretica pravità) viene da masnardiero crudele, eccitato dagli heretici, ferito à morte. Strano portento in vero, che la verità si bella pastorisca l'odio si detestabile e brutto. Lo avvenimento è rappresentato nel principio di folto bosco d'annose quercie e d'altre piante ripieno, che formano de' rami loro ombrosa cortina per riparo del Sole. Quivi il Santo caduto à terra è soprafatto dall'empio homicida, che afferandogli il lembo della cappa, radoppia fieramente il colpo, mentre il Martire glorioso tingendo il dito nel proprio sangue scrive in terra, benche si muora, "Io credo in Dio Padre onnipotente," autenticando fin nell'estremo punto la Christiana Fede. In tanto il Compagno intimorito, percosso anch'egli sopra della testa, tenta con la fuga salvarsi, poiche il timore della morte fà, che si abbandoni nel maggior vopo l'amico, nel cui pallido volto campeggia il timore, e dalla bocca par ch'eschi lo anhelito; mà perche sorano insopportabili i tormenti, mercè dell'humana fragiltà, se la Divina gratia non somministrasse l'aiuto col darci à vedere un raggio della futura gloria, scendono da celeste splendore due vezzosi Angeletti, che arrecano al Martire generoso la palma del trionfo preparatogli nel Cielo; e così bello sono, che sembrano germi di Paradiso; quali ritrasse da un getto di Cupidine, che si crede opera di Fidia, e si tiene dall'universale, che non si possino meglio comporre, proponendosi egli tal'hora l'imitatione delle cose celebri antiche, molto bene da lui conosciute, errando di questo luogo il Vasari, che da Titiano non fossero tali studi praticati, essendo que' bambini condotti nel colorito solo, mà nel disegno à termini di maraviglia.

Viene parimente tenuto, che in questo luogo Titiano dasse il maggiore saggio della sua virtù. Considerisi la collocatione di qualunque cosa ivi rappresentata, ò la qualità del colorito impareggiabile, ammirandosi in quella veramente divina Pittura una mistione de colori, che dimostra la stessa verità, onde ogni parte rappresenta in modo la simiglianza della natura, che alletta l'occhio con industrioso inganno; ò pur considerisi la figura del Santo Martire, nel cui volto si ammirano i pallori della morte ò la fierezza del barbaro homicida, non men dotto per l'intelligenza delle parti e de' muscoli à luoghi loro rassegnati, ò à gli effetti della paura del fuggitivo compagno, à segno, che nell'entrar, che si fà in quell' augusto Tempio, par in effetto di vedere un fatto naturale & il proprio sito d'una boscaglia, ove di lontano nelle cime de' monti (allhor, che sparita l'Aurora bianca e vermiglia) incomincia à sorgere à poco à poco il Sole, strisciando di dorati tratti l'azzurrino Cielo, havendo tolta per apunto quella veduta da monti del Cenedese, che vedeva dalla propria habitatione. Hor per conchiudere, questa pregiatissima tavola vien riputata da ogni intelligente delle migliori sue fatiche, e che in questo luogo egli toccasse l'apice più sublime dell'arte: onde se le può con ragione sottoscrivere quel detto di Zeusi dell'Atleta suo famoso: Chi la invidii ben sia, non che l'imiti.

7. Francesco Scannelli

From Francesco Scannelli, *Il microcosmo della pittura* (1657; reprint, Milan, 1966), 216–7.

Si ritrova pure in Venetia nella Chiesa detta S. Gio. e Polo de' Padri Domenicani la famosissima Tavola del Martirio S. Pietro Martire, Pittura al sicuro della più eccellente bellezza, che in alcun tempo possa dimostrare con suoi più vivi effetti la natura per esprimere in eccellenza il vero. Quivi l'historia vien rapportata all'occhio così adequatamente, che una verita cotanto esatta inorridisce l'applicato spettatore; vedesi nella parte di mezo il Santo, che assalito fieramente dal feroce percussore si ritrova in posto come di fatto abbandonato; già si mirano l'estremità mancanti di spirito, e calore, la faccia languida, e gli horrori della morte vicini, e solo mostrare ne gli occhi ridotta la vita, mentre coll'ultimo spirito affissi al Cielo, già hormai perduto il corpo, fa conoscere stare in un tal punto l'anima per attendere i beni di vita eterna per dove si dimostrano due putti della più vera proportione, e delicata bellezza pronti con la corona, e palma in mano per riconoscere meritamente il gran Campione, il quale con istraordinaria intrepidezza sta sperimentando il martirio, e la morte per Christo, e sua Santa Fede; appare l' Aggressore nell'atto di replicare sopra la testa del Martire moribono nuovi colpi, e per la vista di cosi horrendo spettacolo si vede poco distante il compagno nel primo moto accompagnato dal tutto della più vera, e propria attione, che di già confuso dallo spavento mostra co' più vivi clamori darsi del tutto in preda alla disperata fuga, apportando ad un tempo al riguandante [sic] improvisi effetti non meno di timore, ed horrore, che di maraviglia, e compassione, massime rappresentato in un Bosco, che raffigura al proprio proportionato paese della più facile eccellente, e bella verità, e come estratto della maggior perfettione fa conoscere in epilogo ogni più degna parte, che si possa desidere in un composto della più scielta naturalezza con inventione, dispositione, ed attitudinitali, che ridotte con lo studio, e suprema intelliganza de' colori, mostra le figure al maggior segno della più bella verità, che si venga ad osservare fra l'opere dipinte, e le teste, mani, piedi, col tutto dell'ignudo non meno dell'Aggressore, che de gli Angeletti palesano una particolar idea del vero in eccellenza espresso, e per mostrare, che un tale, come prodigioso historiato, arrechi, per cosi dire, anco vergogna alla stessa natura, basti il concludere, che in fatti sia la più compita, e miglior Tavola, che mai habbia formato con la più egregia mischianza de' colori il gran Maestro Titiano vero Padre della più vera naturalezza...

8. Luigi Scaramuccia

From Luigi Scaramuccia, *Le finezze de' pennnelli italiani ammirate e studiate da Girupeno sotto la scorta e disciplina del Genio di Raffaello d'Urbino* (1674; reprint, Milan, 1965), 95–6.

Mà uno de' maggiori preghi che dar li sentisse fù quello del grand' accordamento del tutto insieme, e del giudito grande, che Titiano haveva usato nella consideratione d'ogni distanza, essendoche da lontano si comprendeva una bellissima macchia, ò vogliam dir massa cagionata dalle gran Piazze de chiari, e de scuri posti à tempo, onde ogni più vero intelligente potesse restarne con molta ragione contento insieme, e stupefatto, e sequendone poi l'avvicinamento potesse conoscere quanto fosse stata la sua grande, ed' artifitiosa Maestria. Quindi il Genio, e Girupeno per una tal visione s'andavano sempre più dichiarando sodifatti, e massime quando oservarono la tenerezza delle Pennellate, e li due Puttini impastati come di Carne, li quali calanti dal Cielo trà fulgidissimi splendori, recano soavi, e brillanti al S. Martire la gloriosa Palma. E da riflessi de i medesimi fulgori impressi nelle Foglie d'una gran Pianta, che meravigliosamente in prima vista d'un bel vago Paese vien situata, gran diletto prederono; Così per l'applicatione introno del Manigoldo assassino, che con l'accompagnamento della Musco-

losa Vita esprime mirabilmente la crudeltà del volto, compita-
mente restarono li due Forastieri edificati, e non pensarono punto
a concludere esser quegli uno de' più bei Quadri, che mai uscissero
dalla valorosa mano del gran Maestro Titiano.

Bibliography

Alberti, Leon Battista. *De Pictura*. Edited by Cecil Grayson. Bari, 1975.

Alpers, Svetlana Leontief. "Ekphrasis and Aesthetic Attitudes in Vasari's *Lives.*" *Journal of the Warburg and Courtauld Institutes* 23 (1960): 190–215.

Andrieux, Maurice. *Daily Life in Venice in the Time of Casanova*. Translated by Mary Fritton. New York and Washington, 1972.

Aretino, Pietro. *Lettere sull'arte*. Edited by Ettore Camesasca, with commentary by Fidenzio Pertile. 3 vols. Milan, 1957–60.

[Aristotle]. *De memoria et reminiscentia*. In *The Works of Aristotle* vol. 3. Translated by John Issac Beare. Oxford, 1908.

Arslan, Edoardo. "Quattro lettere di Pietro Visconti a Gian Pietro Ligari." *Rivista archeologica dell'antica provincia e diocesi di Como* 133 (1952): 63–72.

Bandello, Matteo. *Tutte le opere*. Edited by Francesco Flora. 2 vols. Verona and Milan, 1934–43.

Barcham, William L. *The Religious Paintings of Giambattista Tiepolo: Piety and Tradition in Eighteenth-Century Venice*. Oxford, 1989.

Barolsky, Paul. *Walter Pater's Renaissance*. University Park and London, 1987.

_____. "Metaphorical Meaning in the Sistine Ceiling." *Source: Notes in the History of Art* 9 (1990): 19–22.

Baschet, Armand. "Paul Véronèse au Tribunal du Saint Office, a Venise (1573)." *Gazette des Beaux-Arts* 1st ser., 23 (1867): 378–82.

Bätschmann, Oskar. *Nicolas Poussin: Dialectics of Painting*. London, 1990.

Baxandall, Michael. "Guarino, Pisanello and Manuel Chrysoloras." *Journal of the Warburg and Courtauld Institiutes* 28 (1965): 183–204.

_____. *Giotto and the Orators: Humanist Observers of Painting in Italy and the Discovery of Pictorial Composition, 1350-1450*. Oxford, 1971.

_____. "Alberti and Cristoforo Landino: The Practical Criticism of Painting." In Accademia Nazionale dei Lincei, *Convegno internazionale indetto nel V centenario di Leone Battista Alberti*. Rome, 1974, 143–54.

Bellori, Giovanni Pietro. *Le Vite de' pittori, scultori e architetti moderni*. Edited by Evelina Borea. Turin, 1976.

Bembo, Pietro. *Lettere I (1492-1507)*. Edited by Ernesto Travi. Bologna, 1987.

Berenson, Bernard. *Venetian Painting Chiefly before Titian at the Exhibition of Venetian Art*. The New Gallery, London, 1895.

_____. *Venetian Painting in America*. New York, 1916.

Blunt, Anthony. "Poussin's Notes on Painting." *Journal of the Warburg and Courtauld Institutes* 1 (1937–1938): 344–51.

_____. *Artistic Theory in Italy, 1450-1600*. Oxford, 1940.

_____, ed. *Nicholas Poussin: Lettres et propos sur l'art*. Paris, 1964.

Borghini, Raffaello. *Il Riposo*. 1584. Reprint. Edited by Marco Rosci. 2 vols. Milan, 1967.

Boschini, Marco. *La carta del navegar pittoresco*. Edited by Anna Pallucchini. Venice, 1966.

Braunfels, Wolfgang, "Giovanni Bellini's Paradiesgärtlein." *Das Munster* 9 (1956): 1–13.

Brown, Clifford M. and Anna Maria Lorenzoni. *Isabella d'Este and Lorenzo da Pavia: Documents for the History of Art and Culture in Renaissance Mantua*. Geneva, 1982.

Carrier, David. "Ekphrasis and Interpretation: Two Modes of Art History Writing." *British Journal of Aesthetics* 27 (1987): 20–31.

_____. *Poussin's Paintings: A Study in Art-Historical Methodology*. University Park, 1993.

Casella, Maria Teresa and Giovanni Pozzi. *Francesco Colonna: biografia e opere*. 2 vols. Padua, 1959.

Cennini, Cennino. *Il libro dell'arte o trattato della pittura*. Edited by Fernando Tempesta. Milan, 1975.

Castelfranchi Vegas, Liana. *International Gothic Art In Italy*. Translated by B. D. Phillips, revised by D. Talbot Rice. London, 1968.

Chantelou, Paul Fréart de. "Journal de voyage du Cavalier Bernin in France." Edited by Ludovic Lalanne. *Gazette des Beaux-Arts* 2nd ser. 23, (1881): 271–80.

Chastel, André. "The Arts During the Renaissance." In *The Renaissance: Essays In Interpretation*, London and New York, 1982, 227–71.

_____. "Roberto Longhi: Il genio dell'*ekphrasis*." In *L'arte di scrivere sull'arte: Roberto Longhi nella cultura del nostro tempo*. Rome, 1982, 56–65.

_____. *Art of the Italian Renaissance*. Translated by Linda and Peter Murray. New York, 1988.

Colombier, Pierre du, ed. *Lettres du Poussin*. Paris, 1929.

Colonna, Francesco. *See* Pozzi, Giovanni and Lucia A. Ciapponi.

Cropper, Elizabeth. "Poussin and Leonardo: Evidence from the Zaccolini MSS." *Art Bulletin* 62 (1980): 570–83.

_____. *The Ideal of Painting: Pietro Testa's Düsseldorf Notebook*. Princeton, 1984.

Crowe, Joseph Archer and Giovanni Battista Cavalcaselle. *A History of Painting in North Italy*. 2 vols. London, 1871.

D'Argaville, Brian T. "Inquisition and Metamorphosis: Paolo Veronese and the 'Ultima Cena' of 1573." *RACAR: Revue d'art canadienne / Canadian Art Review* 16 (1989): 43–8.

Delaney, Susan. "The Inconography of Giovanni Bellini's *Sacred Allegory*." *Art Bulletin* 59 (1977): 331–5.

Dolce, Lodovico. *Dialogo della pittura, intitolato l'Aretino*. In *Trattati d'arte del cinquecento*, edited by Paola Barocchi. 3 vols. Bari, 1960, 140–206.

Eisler, Colin. "In Detail: Bellini's *Saint Francis*." *Portfolio* (April-May 1979): 18–23.

Fehl, Philipp. "Veronese and the Inquisition: A Study of the Subject-Matter of the so-called 'Feast in the House of Levi'." *Gazette des Beaux-Arts* 6th ser., 58 (1961): 325–54.

_____. "Veronese's Decorum: Notes on the 'Marriage at Cana'." In *Art the Ape of Nature: Studies in Honor of H. W. Janson*, edited by Moshe Barasch, Lucy Freeman Sandler and Patricia Egan. New York, 1981, 341–65.

Fehl, Philipp and Marilyn Perry. "Painting and the Inquisition at Venice: Three Forgotten Files." In *Interpretazioni veneziane: Studi di storia dell'arte in onore di Michelangelo Muraro*, edited by David Rosand. Venice, 1984, 371–83.

Fiocco, Giuseppe. "Michele Giambono." *Venezia* 1 (1920): 206–242.

Fleming, John V. *From Bonaventure to Bellini: An Essay in Franciscan Exegesis.* Princeton, 1982.

Fletcher, Jennifer M. "The Provenance of Bellini's Frick 'St. Francis'." *Burlingon Magazine* 114 (1972): 206–14.

Fogolari, Gino. "Il processo dell'Inquisizione a Paolo Veronese." *Archivio veneto* 17 (1935): 378-9.

Freedberg, Sydney J. *Painting in Italy, 1500-1600. The Pelican History of Art.* Baltimore, 1975.

[Frick Collection.] *The Frick Collection: An Illustrated Catalogue.* 7 vols. New York, 1968.

Friedlander, Walter. *Nicolas Poussin, A New Approach.* New York, n.d.

Gaye, Giovanni and Alfred von Reumont, eds. *Carteggio inedito d'artisti dei secoli XIV. XV. XVI.* 3 vols. Florence, 1839–1840.

Gilbert, Creighton. "On Subject and Non-Subject in Italian Renaissance Pictures." *Art Bulletin* 34 (1952): 202–16.

_____. "Last Suppers and Their Refectories." In *The Pursuit of Holiness in Late Medieval and Renaissance Religion*, edited by Charles Trinkhaus and Heiko A. Oberman. Leiden, 1974, 371–402.

Ginori Lisci, Leonardo. *The Palazzi of Florence: Their History and Art.* Translated by Jennifer Grillo. 2 vols. Florence, 1985.

Goffen, Rona. *Giovanni Bellini.* New Haven and London, 1989.

Gombrich, Ernst H. "The Leaven of Criticism in Renaissance Art." In *Art, Science, and History in the Renaissance*, edited by Charles S. Singleton. Baltimore, 1967, 3–42.

_____. *The Sense of Order: A Study in the Psychology of Decorative Art.* Ithaca, 1979.

Gould, Cecil. "Veronese's Greatest Feast: The Inter-action of Iconographic and Aesthetic Factors." *Arte Veneta* 43 (1989–90): 85–88.

Harris, Ann Sutherland. *Andrea Sacchi.* Princeton, 1977.

Hartt, Frederick. *Italian Renaissance Art.* 3rd ed. Englewood Cliffs, 1987.

Haskell, Francis. *Patrons and Painters: A Study in the Relations Between Italian Art and Society in the Age of the Baroque.* 2nd ed. New Haven and London,1980.

Hendy, Phillip. *European and American Paintings in the Isabella Stewart Gardner Museum.* Boston, 1974.

Hetzer, Theodor. "Francisco Goya and the Crisis of Art around 1800." In *Goya in Perspective*, edited by Fred Licht. Englewood Cliffs, 1973, 92–113.

Hibbard, Howard. *Caravaggio*. New York, 1983.

Holt, Elizabeth G., ed. *A Documentary History of Art*. 2 vols. Princeton, 1982.

Howard, Deborah. "Giorgione's *Tempesta* and Titian's *Assunta* in the Context of the Cambrai Wars." *Art History* 8 (1985): 271–89.

Huse, Norbert. *Studien zu Giovanni Bellini*. Berlin and New York, 1972.

Jouanny, Charles, ed. *Correspondance de Nicolas Poussin*. Paris, 1911.

Kaplan, Paul H. D. "The Storm of War: the Paduan Key to Giorgione's *Tempesta*." *Art History* 9 (1985): 405–27.

_____. "Veronese's Last 'Last Supper'." *Arte veneta* 41 (1987): 51-62.

Knox, George. *Giambattista and Domenico Tiepolo: A Catalogue Raisonné of the Chalk Drawings*. 2 vols. Oxford, 1980.

Land, Norman E. "Michele Giambono's 'Coronation of the Virgin' for S. Agnese in Venice: A New Proposal." *Burlington Magazine* 119 (1977): 167–74.

_____. "Two Panels by Michele Giambono and Some Observations on St. Francis and the Man of Sorrows in Fifteenth-Century Venetian Painting." *Studies in Iconography* 6 (1980): 29–51.

_____. "A New Proposal for Michele Giambono's Altarpiece for S. Michele in S. Daniele in Friuli." *Pantheon* 4 (1981): 304–9.

_____. "The Master of the San Marino 'Saints' and Other Followers of Michele Giambono." *Acta Historiae Artium* 28 (1982): 23–38.

_____. "Jacopo Bellini's Lost *St. Michael* and a Possible Date for Pisanello." *Zeitschrift für Kunstgeschichte* 45 (1982): 282–6.

_____. "A New Panel by Michele Giambono and a Reconstructed Altarpiece." *Apollo* 119 (1984): 160–5.

_____. "Ekphrasis and Imagination: Some Observations on Pietro Aretino's Art Criticism." *Art Bulletin* 68 (1986): 209–12.

Lattanzi, Marco and Stefano Cotellacci. "Studi belliniani: proposte iconologiche per la Sacra allegoria degli Uffizi." In *Giorgione e la cultura veneta tra '400 e '500: mito, allegoria, analisi iconologica*. Rome, 1981, 59–79.

Lee, Vernon. *See* Paget, Violet.

Leonardo da Vinci. *See* Richter, Jean Paul.

Levey, Michael. *Giambattista Tiepolo: His Life and Art*. New Haven and London, 1986.

Lomazzo, Gian Paolo. *Scritti sulle arti*. Edited by Roberto Paolo Ciardi. 2 vols. Florence, 1973–5.

Ludwig, Gustav. "Giovanni Bellini's sogenannte Madonna am see in den Uffizien: eine religiose Allegorie." *Jahrbuch der Königlich Preussischen Kunstsammlungen* 23 (1902): 163–86.

Marconi, Sandra Moschini. *Gallerie dell'Accademia di Venezia: Opere d'arte del secolo XVI*. Rome, 1962.

Mariuz, Adriano. "The Drawings of Giambattista Tiepolo." In *Masterpieces of Eighteenth-Century Venetian Drawing*. Translated by David Smith. London and New York, 1983, 21–70.

Marle, Raimond van. *The Development of the Italian Schools of Painting*. 19 vols. The Hague, 1923–38.

Meilman, Patricia. "Titian's Saint Peter Martyr and the Development of Altar Painting in Renaissance Venice." (Ph. D. Diss., Columbia University,

1989.)

Meiss, Millard. *Painting in Florence and Siena after the Black* Death. Princeton, 1951.

_____. "Jan van Eyck and the Italian Renaissance." In *Venezia e l'Europa: Atti del XVIII congresso internazionale de storia dell'arte, 1955*. Venice, 1956, 58–69.

_____. " 'Highlands' in the Lowlands: Jan van Eyck, the Master of Flémalle and the Franco-Italian Tradition." *Gazette des Beaux Arts* 57 (1961): 273–314.

_____."Giovanni Bellini's *St. Francis.*" *Saggi e Memorie di storia dell'arte* 3 (1963): 11–30.

_____. *Giovanni Bellini's Saint Francis in the Frick Collection.* New York, 1964.

_____."Giovanni Bellini's 'St. Francis'." *Burlington Magazine* 107 (1966): 27.

_____. "Sleep in Venice: Ancients Myths and Renaissance Proclivities." *Proceedings of the American Philiosophical Society* 110 (1966): 348–86.

_____. *The Painter's Choice: Problems in the Interpretation of Renaissance Art.* New York, 1976.

Oberhuber, Konrad. *Poussin: The Early Years in Rome.* New York, 1988.

Osmund, Percy H. *Paolo Veronese: His Career and Work.* London, 1927.

Ottonelli, Giovanni Domenico and Pietro Berrettini [Pietro da Cortona, pseud.].*Trattato della pittura e scultura: uso e abuso loro.* 1652. Reprint. Edited by Vittoria Casale. Treviso, 1973.

Paget, Violet. [Vernon Lee, pseud.]."The Imaginative Art of the Renaissance." In *Renaissance Fancies and Studies.* New York and London, 1896, 67–133.

Palladino, Lora Ann. "Pietro Aretino: Orator and Art Theorist." (Ph.D. Diss., Yale University, 1981.)

Pallucchini, Ridolfo. *La pittura veneziano del Trecento.* Venice and Rome, 1964.

Panofsky, Erwin. "The History of Art as a Humanistic Discipline." In *Meaning in the Visual Arts.* New York, 1955, 1–25.

Passerini, Giovanni L., ed. *I Fioretti del glorioso messere Santo Francesco e de' suoi frati.* Florence, 1919.

Pater, Walter. *The Renaissance.* Edited by Donald L. Hill. Berkeley, Los Angeles and London, 1980.

Pignatti, Terisio. *Veronese.* 2 vols. Venice, 1976.

Pino, Paolo. *Dialogo di pittura.* In *Trattati d'arte del Cinquecento fra manierismo e controriforma,* edited by Paola Barocchi. 3 vols. Bari, 1960, 1:93–139.

Piper, David. *Looking at Art.* New York, 1984.

[Pliny, The Elder.] *The Elder Pliny's Chapters on the History of Art.* Translated by K. Jex-Blake. Chicago, 1968.

Popham, Arthur E. "A Book of Drawings of the School of Benezzo Gozzoli." *Old Master Drawings* 4 (1929–30): 53–4.

Posner, Donald. "The Picture of Painting in Poussin's Self-Portrait." In *Essays in the History of Art Presented to Rudolf Wittkower,* edited by Douglas Fraser, Howard Hibbard and Milton J. Lewine. London, 1967, 200-3.

Poussin, Nicolas. *See* Blunt, Anthony; Colombier, Pierre du; and Jouanny, Charles.

Pozzi, Giovanni and Lucia A. Ciapponi, eds. *Hypnerotomachia Poliphili.* 2

vols. Padua, 1964.

Rasmo, Niccolò. "La sacra conversazione belliniana degli Uffizi e il problema della sua comprensione." *Carro minore* 5–6 (1946): 229–40.

Rearick, W. R. *The Art of Paolo Veronese, 1528–1588.* Washington, D. C. and London, 1988.

Riccòmini, Eugenio. "Il capolavoro di Tiziano non era bruciato," *Giornale dell' arte* 7 (October 1989): 1–2.

Richter, Jean Paul, ed. and trans. *The Literary Works of Leonardo da Vinci.* 2 vols. 3rd ed. New York, 1970.

Ridolfi, Carlo. *Le maraviglie dell'arte.* 1648. Reprint. Edited by Detlev von Hadeln. 2 vols. Rome, 1965.

_____. *The Life of Tintortetto.* Translated by Catherine Enggass, with an introduction by Robert Enggass. University Park and London, 1984.

Robertson, Giles. *Giovanni Bellini.* Oxford, 1968.

Robinson, F. W. "Rembrandt's Influence in Eighteenth-Century Venice." *Nederlands Kunsthistorisch Jaarboek* 18 (1967): 167–96.

Rosand, David. *Titian.* New York, 1978.

_____. *Painting in Cinquecento Venice: Titian, Veronese, Tintoretto.* New Haven and London, 1982.

_____. "Ekphrasis and the Renaissance of Painting: Observations on Alberti's Third Book." In *Florilegium Columbianum: Essays in Honor of Paul Oskar Kristeller*, edited by Karl-Ludwig Selig and Robert Somerville. New York, 1987, 147–63.

Sansovino, Francesco. *Venetia: città nobilissima et singolare.* Venice, 1581.

Scannelli, Francesco. *Il microcosmo della pittura.* 1657. Reprint. Edited by Guido Guibbini. Milan, 1965.

Scaramuccia, Luigi. *Le finezze de' pennelli italiani ammirate e studiate da Girupeno sotto la scorta e disciplina del Genio di Raffaello d'Urbino.* 1674. Reprint. Edited by Guido Guibbini. Milan, 1965.

Schapiro, Meyer. "On Some Problems in the Semiotics of Visual Art: Field and Vehicle in Image-Signs." *Semiotica* 1 (1969): 223–42.

Schlosser, Julius von. *La letteratura artistica.* 1964. Reprint. Edited by Otto Kurz. Translated by Filippo Rossi. Florence, 1977.

Schroeder, Henry Joseph, trans. *Canons and Decrees of the Council of Trent.* Saint Louis and London, 1941.

Settis, Salvatore. *La "Tempesta" interpretata: Giorgione, i committenti, il soggetto.* Turin, 1978.

_____. *Giorgione's Tempest: Interpreting the Hidden Subject.* Translated by Ellen Bianchini. Chicago, 1990.

Shapley, Fern Rusk. *Paintings from the Samuel H. Kress Collection: Italian Schools, XV-XVI.* 2 vols. London, 1968.

Sheard, Wendy S.. "Giorgione's *Tempesta*: External vs. Internal Texts," *Italian Culture* 4 (1983): 145–58.

Sinding-Larsen, Staale. *Christ in the Council Hall, Studies in the Religious Iconography of the Venetian Republic.* Acta ad Archaeologiam et Artium Historiam Pertinentia, V. Rome, 1974.

Smart, Alastair. "The *Speculum Perfectionis* and Bellini's *St. Francis.*" *Apollo,* 97 (1973): 470–6.

Steer, John. Review of Millard Meiss, *Giovanni Bellini's Saint Francis in the Frick Collection*. New York, 1964. In *Burlington Magazine* 107 (1965): 533–4.

Stokes, Adrian. "Painting, Giorgione and Barbaro." *The Criterion* 9 (1929–30): 482–500.

Summers, David. *Michelangelo and the Language of Art*. Princeton, 1981.

_____. *The Judgment of Sense: Renaissance Naturalism and the Rise of Aesthetics*. Cambridge, 1987.

Symonds, John Addington. "On an Altar-piece by Tiepolo." In *In the Key of Blue and Other Prose Essays*. New York and London, 1918 [1st edition, 1893], 41-53.

_____."Venetian Painting." *Westminster Review* 196 (April 1873): 183–190.

Tervarent, Guy de. *Attributs et symboles dans l'art profane, 1450-1600*. Geneva, 1959.

Turner, A. Richard. *The Vision of Landscape in Renaissance Italy*. Princeton, 1966.

Vasari, Giorgio. *Le vite de' più eccellenti pittori, scultori ed archiettori*. Edited by Gaetano Milanesi. 9 vols. Florence, 1906.

Venturi, Lionello. *Le origini della pittura veneziana*. Venice, 1907.

Verdier, Philippe. "L'Allegoria della Misericordia e della Giustizia di Giambellino agli Uffizi." *Atti dell'istituto veneto di scienza, lettere ed arti* 109 (1952–53): 97–116.

Verheyen, Egon. *The Paintings in the 'Studiolo' of Isabella d'Este at Mantua*. New York, 1971.

Weinberg, Bernard. *A History of Literary Criticism in the Italian Renaissance*. 2 vols. Chicago, 1961.

Welsford, Enid. *The Fool: His Social and Literary History*. Gloucester [Mass.], 1966.

Wethey, Harold E. *The Paintings of Titian, I: The Religious Paintings*. London, 1969.

Wilde, Johannes. *Venetian Art: From Bellini to Titian*. Oxford, 1974.

Winner, Mattias. "Poussin's Selbbildnis im Louvre als Kunsttheoretische Allegorie." *Römisches Jahrbuch für Kunstgeschichte* 20 (1983):410–49.

1 Giorgione: *Tempest*. Venice, Gallerie dell'Accademia.
(Alinari/Art Resource)

2 Michele Giambono: *St. Michael Archangel*.
Florence, Berenson Collection. (Reproduced by permission of the
President and Fellows of Harvard College)

3 Michele Giambono: *Madonna and Child*.
Rome, Galleria Nazionale. (Alinari/Art Resource)

4 Michele Giambono: *Man of Sorrows*.
Padua, Museo Civico.

5 Michele Giambono: *St. Michael*
(detail: St. James Polyptych). Venice, Gallerie dell'Accademia.

6 Lorenzo Veneziano: *Annunciation to the Virgin*.
Venice, Gallerie dell'Accademia. (Alinari/Art Resource)

154

7 Jacobello and Pierpaolo dalle Masegne: *Crucifixion with Saints.*
Venice, Church of San Marco. (Alinari/Art Resource)

155

8 Michele Giambono: *Madonna and Child*. Bassano del Grappa, Museo Civico. (Alinari/Art Resource)

9 Gentile da Fabriano: *Virgin and Child* (fragment).
Florence, Berenson Collection. (Reproduced by permission of the
President and Fellows of Harvard College)

10 Jacopo Bellini: *Madonna and Child with Donor.*
Paris, Louvre. (Giraudon/Art Resource)

11 Michele Giambono: *Veil of Veronica*.
Pavia, Museo Civico. (Alinari/Art Resource)

12 Jacobello del Fiore: *Justice-Venice*.
Venice, Gallerie dell'Accademia. (Alinari/Art Resource)

160

13 Giovanni Bellini. *St. Francis.*
New York, Frick Collection. (Copyright The Frick Collection, New York)

161

14 Paolo Veneziano: *Stigmatization of St. Francis* (detail: Sta. Chiara
Altarpiece). Venice, Gallerie dell'Accademia. (O. Böhm)

15 Michele Giambono: *Stigmatization of St. Francis.*
Venice, Cini Collection.

163

16 Domenico Veneziano: *Stigmatization of St. Francis*.
Washington, National Gallery of Art, Samuel H. Kress Collection.

17 Giovanni Bellini. *Stigmatization of St. Francis*
(detail: Pesaro Polyptych). Pesaro, Museo Civico. (Alinari / Art Resource)

18 Jan van Eyck: *Stigmatization of St. Francis.*
Turin, Galleria Sabauda. (Alinari / Art Resource)

19 Giovanni Bellini: *Sacred Allegory.*
Florence, Uffizi Gallery. (Alinari / Art Resource)

167

20 Lorenzo Lotto: *A Maiden's Dream*.
Washington, National Gallery of Art, Samuel H. Kress Collection.

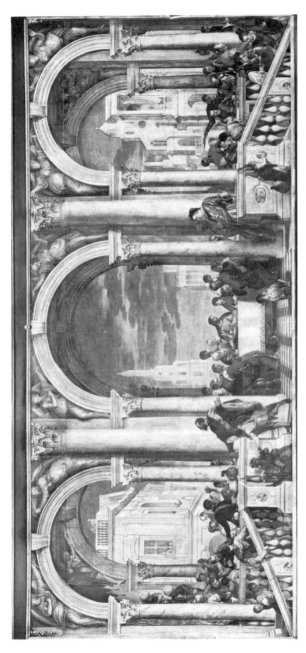

21 Paolo Veronese: *Feast in the House of Levi.*
Venice, Gallerie dell'Accademia. (Alinari/Art Resource)

22 Paolo Veronese: *Feast in the House of the Pharisee*.
Turin, Pinacoteca. (Alinari/Art Resource)

170

23 Paolo Veronese: *Wedding Feast at Cana.*
Paris, Louvre. (Giraudon / Art Resource)

24 Paolo Veronese: *Feast in the House of Simon the Leper.*
Paris, Louvre. (Giraudon/Art Resource)

25 Paolo Veronese: *Feast in the House of the Pharisee*.
Milan, Brera. (Alinari/Art Resource)

26 Michelangelo: *Last Judgment*.
Rome, Vatican, Sistine Chapel. (Alinari/Art Resource)

27 Martino Rota: *Martyrdom of St. Peter Martyr* (engraving after Titian's lost painting). New York, Metropolitan Museum of Art (Purchase Joseph Pulitzer Bequest, 1917).

28 Titian: *Ecce Homo*. St. Louis, St. Louis Museum of Art.

29 Titian: *Mary Magdalen.*
Florence, Pitti Gallery. (Alinari / Art Resource)

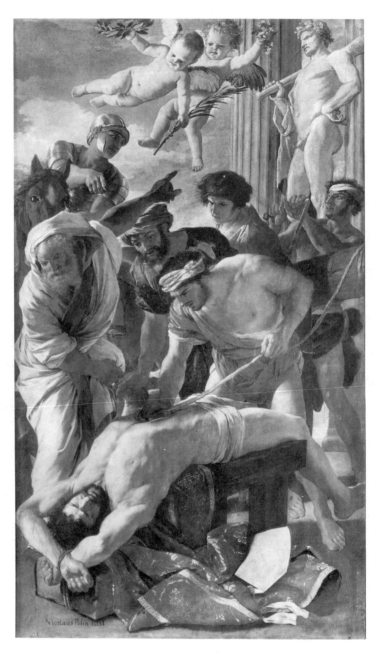

30 Nicolas Poussin: *Martyrdom of St. Erasmus.*
Rome, Vatican, Pinacoteca. (Alinari/Art Resource)

31 Nicolas Poussin: *Self-Portrait*.
Paris, Louvre. (Giraudon / Art Resource)

179

32 Titian: *Portrait of a Bearded Man*.
London, National Gallery.

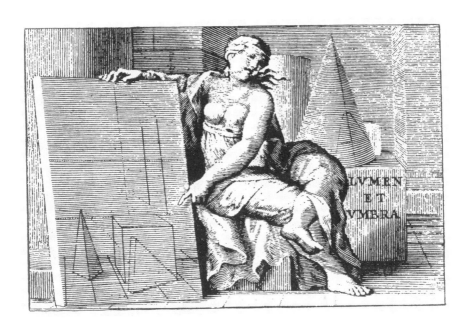

33 Fronticepiece to the vita of Nicolas Poussin in G. P. Bellori,
Le Vite…, Rome, 1673.

34 Giambattista and Giandomenico Tiepolo: *Crucifixion*,
St. Louis, St. Louis Art Museum.

35 Paolo Veronese: *Crucifixion*.
Paris, Louvre. (Giraudon/Art Resource)

36 Giotto: *Lamentation*.
Padua, Arena Chapel. (Alinari/Art Resource)

Index

References are to page or plate (*pl.*) numbers